Alison Rice is a freelance travel writer and broadcaster. When envious friends say 'It must be like being on holiday full time', she admits that the job does have its perks. But she also points out that she has spent more time than most waiting around in airports (about five and a half weeks of her life, she estimates). And, that while she has stayed in some of the world's best hotels, she has also experienced some of the worst.

For all the grim experiences and disappointments she has never lost her yen for travelling. Her honest and unbiased reports of holiday destinations – the good, the bad and the downright lousy – have made her one of the most entertaining and useful travel writers.

After a career as a magazine editor and a Radio One presenter, Alison decided to go it alone in 1983. Since then she has been TV-AM's travel editor, has presented 'Daytime Trippers' on BBC TV's *Daytime Live* and writes for the *Mail on Sunday*, the *Observer* and the *Guardian* as well as a variety of magazines including *Chat*, *Prima* and *Parents*. She is the author of *Talking Turkey* published in 1989.

Also by Alison Rice

Talking Turkey

ALISON RICE

Travel Tips and Holiday Hints

Mandarin

A Mandarin Paperback

TRAVEL TIPS AND HOLIDAY HINTS

First published in Great Britain 1990
by Mandarin Paperbacks
Michelin House, 81 Fulham Road, London SW3 6RB

Mandarin is an imprint of the Octopus Publishing Group

Copyright © 1990 by Alison Rice

A CIP catalogue record for this book
is available from the British Library
ISBN 0 7493 0269 0

Phototypeset by Input Typesetting Ltd, London
Printed in Great Britain
by Cox & Wyman Ltd, Reading

To Jeffery Pike *with love*

• Contents

• Acknowledgements

I would dearly like to thank every traveller and travel organ-isation who has offered me advice and help throughout all my travels. But if I had the wit to remember them all and to list them all here, you'd have needed a wheelbarrow to carry this book home. Instead I shall have to pick out just some of the organisations and individuals who went out of their way to help me with some points that were specifically destined for this book.

My grateful thanks to the people at the AA, Saga, RADAR, the Holiday Care Service and the BAA.

I am also in the debt of Denita and Martin Wilson and Jackie Weatherstone for their common-sense advice and holiday hints.

I confess that this book only managed to see the light of day because of the infinite patience and talent of Jeffery Pike who knocked it into shape for me.

The idea for the book came from Heather Jeeves, whose encouragement, friendliness and valuable business sense make her the very best of agents.

● Introduction

Every holiday you ever take should be perfect. You save hard enough to pay for your holidays and you deserve a break from work and humdrum daily routine. A good holiday should set you up for the rest of the year. It should be exciting or relaxing. Or both. In fact, a proper holiday should be whatever you want it to be. When I rule the world, holidays will be on the National Health.

It's a great pity then that many holidays turn out to be expensive disappointments. Perhaps you found out the hard way that no one in the country would take credit cards and you ran out of cash on the fifth day. Perhaps you had to spend two weeks in Spain in one set of clothes because your suitcase took a trip to Italy. Or maybe you were attacked non-stop by kamikaze mosquitoes. Holiday problems can be niggling annoyances or major catastrophes. Either way, some inside information might have helped you cope. Or it could have stopped you getting in the mess in the first place.

And that quite simply is what this book is offering: hints and tips.

I don't pretend to provide a magic recipe for the perfect holiday. There isn't one. Instead I've collected titbits of information that answer some often-asked questions – the sort with answers that are hard to come by unless you make travelling and holidays your full-time job. And I've rounded up a host of offbeat traveller's tips – answers to questions you might never have thought of asking.

Dip into the book, or read it from cover to cover. Follow

the hints and tips faithfully, or ignore them. But whatever you do, have yourself a wonderful holiday.

● Choosing the Right Holiday

Holidays are different from anything else we ever spend money on. You can never buy a holiday in the same way that you buy a coat, a car or a washing machine. For a start, you can't have a free try-out before you agree to buy. And when you've bought the holiday and taken it and hated it, you can't take it back to the shop and ask if they would mind changing it for a different one please.

What do you want? The first rule for avoiding disappointment sounds obvious, but it's worth stating. Before you even open a brochure, you must ask yourself *why* you're going on holiday.

There are as many valid reasons for buying a holiday as there are flies at a beach barbecue. We all want different things from our holidays. Most of us want a proper break from work and daily routine. We want to relax, to spend time with our partners and to make new friends. Sometimes we want to look at famous historical sights or art treasures. Sometimes we want to indulge in a favourite pastime – skiing or scuba-diving or eating and drinking. Often we want to see for ourselves what life is like in other countries. Most of us also know how we want the weather to be: hot and dry.

People can have very private reasons for travelling. Couples sometimes book a holiday together in the hope that the break will 'save' their marriage (and it sometimes works). Other couples fly off to celebrate being together or because they plan to start a family. Singles leave home for two weeks because they hope to find a partner. We go off on holiday to help us get over a broken romance or the death of someone we love, or to make us feel better when we've been ill. Some people spend money on holidays because they like boasting about their exotic journeys and showing off their tans when they get back. And many of us go away every year because, when you can afford it, that's what you do every year: have a holiday.

But the Joneses are going to Nepal: There are plenty of reasons why holidays don't turn out as perfect as you'd hoped (on pages 229–235 you'll find out what you can do about some of them). But the most common cause for holiday complaints, like it or not, is simply that you chose the wrong holiday.

List your preferences: When you're looking around for holiday ideas, ask yourself what sort of holiday you *really* prefer. Make a list of all the things you want – and those you don't want – from your holiday.

- Do you enjoy new experiences or are you more relaxed when your meals and your surroundings are just like at home?
- Is where you sleep when you're away very important to you, or is your bedroom just somewhere to clean your teeth, hang your clothes, and catch some sleep before the dawn?
- Do you enjoy meeting new people or do you prefer time to yourself and with the people you're holidaying with? Or put it another way: will you be able to bear the company of just your partner day in and day out for two weeks, or do you need the distraction of other faces?
- Do you want to be tied to a hotel's schedule or do you prefer to organise your own routine and eat when and where you choose?
- Are you happy to be responsible for buying and cooking food for the family, or do you want a holiday precisely to get away from all that?

- Would you find staying among people of a very different culture stimulating or stressful?
- If you have children, will they settle for the garlic sardines and jug of plonk you so loved on your honeymoon? Or will you all be happier if there's pizza, chips and Cokes on tap?
- Will the kids want other children to play with? Will you be happy and rested being with them all the time or would you like there to be children's 'clubs' on hand? An apartment with a pool sounds lovely but are you prepared to watch very young children their every waking minute to stop them toddling off into the deep end?

Put your likes and dislikes in order of importance and keep your list with you as you shop. Then ask yourself:

Why are you buying a holiday: because you want a break, you want a suntan, you want a rest, you want to impress your friends?

How much can you afford? When I go into a supermarket with a short shopping list, somehow I get to the check-out with a trolley-load of stuff I've just discovered I 'need'. It can be the same with buying holidays. Except that when the shop assistant totals up my load I know that that's the final bill. With a holiday, you have to remember to add all the 'invisible' costs, like getting passports and visas, insurance, your spending money, the cost of getting to the airport. And probably some new clothes and all that suntan cream.

You need to find out what the cost of living is going to be like. How much is a meal going to cost you out there? (Don't be afraid to ask anyone you know who's been there recently.) On second thoughts, if we added up the real cost of a break, I doubt that any of us would ever get further than the local leisure centre.

When can you go? Are you tied to the same holiday dates every year or do you travel away every August because of tradition? The busiest and most expensive times are usually from mid-July to the end of August. If you're not tied to school or work holidays, consider going away before or after the peak periods. Holidays to Europe are nearly always cheaper outside the high season. There are fewer people travelling, too, which means more relaxed journeys. And it's worth remembering that in places like Greece and southern Spain the scenery is greener and prettier before the hottest summer months.

Holidays over the Christmas, Easter and half-term holidays sell out very quickly. Some places and some air routes are fully booked for Christmas by 6 January!

In far-away places the peak holiday time isn't necessarily our summer. The most popular times and the highest prices all depend on the local weather patterns. (As part of a trip to Shanghai, I got an excellent price for a stay by a beach in Thailand. No wonder. When I got there the monsoon was in full swing.)

School holidays need not be a restriction on your choice of dates. Children are allowed to take two weeks a year off school for a family holiday. You might feel that for young children two weeks in a foreign country is as good an education as the two weeks missed from class.

But don't forget that in places which are not open to tourists all year round, like Greece and Yugoslavia, you will find that at the very beginning and the very end of the season the entertainment spots, the cafés and the pools are closed. Hotels and resorts use their quieter months to get on with their building works.

Who do you know who's been? One of the best pointers for a holiday – better than any brochure or travel agent – is a recommendation from someone who's been there, done that. Provided, of course, it's someone who shares the same ideas as you about what makes a good holiday. One person's idea of a nice hotel might be someone else's idea of a dump. But if you have a friend or relative who has the same standards as you, and looks for the same things from a holiday, there's no shame in booking exactly the same package as they had. If they enjoyed it, the chances are you will too.

When to book? Every year the travel people scream at us to book our holidays early. They warn us that there will be no holidays left after Easter and most certainly no late bargains. Well, they would say that, wouldn't they? The earlier we book, the longer they have our deposits in the bank.

However, if no one books early, the travel companies can, and often do, cancel flights and bookings for accommodation, leaving us with little holiday choice. If enough people book a certain package for the company to keep the holiday running, but not enough to fill all the seats on the plane, then some weeks before the departure date it becomes worth their while to offer the package at a discount, just to sell the remaining places. The nearer it gets to the holiday date, the bigger the discount. Any income is better than none because, once the plane takes off, an empty seat is worthless.

It's all a bit of a gamble, really, and what you need to know is: the later you book, the more flexible you need to be.

Booking early: If you're tied to definite holiday dates and you're particular about where you stay, where you fly from and when, you should book as early as possible. (Mind you, this still doesn't always guarantee you'll get the holiday you booked, see page 229.)

Holidays offering good value family hotels in popular resorts during the school summer holidays sell out the week they are put on sale. The later you leave it, the less choice you'll have.

If you book early, *do* buy your holiday insurance at the same time. Make sure you have a policy that will cover you if you have to cancel later because of unexpected circumstances.

Booking late: Last-minute bookings can be fine if you really don't mind which resort you stay in – or even which country – and if you're not bothered about exactly when you travel.

You must realise the implications of a 'blind date' late booking. Blind date holidays usually have snazzy titles like

Square Deal or Price Beater: they offer low prices for holidays you take at short notice. You know in advance which airport you'll be flying from and which resort or which area you'll be staying in. You also know what grade of accommodation you'll be staying in and usually what sort – hotel or self-catering apartment. However, the holiday company chooses exactly where you stay and often you're not told until you arrive at the foreign airport.

These 'blind date' cut-price offers have generated an unusually high number of complaints. They're fine if you really are carefree enough to take pot luck with your accommodation. The standard of where you stay will be guaranteed but you have no come-back whatsoever if it's not to your liking. If you find your room is the wrong side of a motorway from the beach, or you're two miles from any night-life or you have to sleep one floor above a disco, don't say I didn't warn you.

It's stupid to be smart: Beware of choosing a holiday as a fashion accessory, going to a country just because it's a 'smart' thing to do. If it's not really your kind of place, you'll have a miserable time – and that's a high price to pay for showing off to the neighbours.

In fact, there's a lot of snobbery wrapped up with holidays. If only I had a fiver for every tourist I've met who likes to proclaim, 'Of course, I never fly charter.' More fool them. Charter flights can be so much cheaper than schedule flights – give me the extra pocket money every time.

Or then there's the holidaymaker on an African safari who isn't really interested in animals, or the person trudging round Far Eastern temples who doesn't really care about exotic architecture or religions. They're just doing it because they think it's a smart thing to do – you don't win so many points at the squash club with snapshots of the Costa Blanca.

Fact or fiction? Holiday brochures make fascinating reading. Have you ever compared how different companies describe the same places? By law, there's a limit to just how far holiday brochures can stretch the truth before they become illegal. But sometimes they come alarmingly close to being pure fiction.

It's not what brochures say that you should note. It's what they *don't* say. If a certain beach is lovely, with good sand, every brochure will harp on about it. What about the beach resorts where the sand gets no special mention? Is there any sand? Is there any beach?

Brochures are advertisements: they exist to sell you holidays. If a hotel or resort is at the end of a noisy airport runway (like, for instance, Kanoni in Corfu), don't expect the company to tell you. Look instead for the tell-tale transfer time from the airport to the hotel. If it's only ten minutes, pack your earplugs.

Just because every person in every photograph in a brochure is tanned and wearing swimming togs, that doesn't mean that a place is always hot. If the weather is important to you, check up elsewhere on the average temperatures and rainfall.

However much a company might harp on about 'telling it like it is', no brochure is going to describe accommodation as 'tatty, tiny, grubby and smells of drains and cooking oil from the café underneath. Run by a surly couple who don't speak English'. Instead, you must expect to read 'a long-established, family-run place that's small and very handy for the local restaurant'. Just as a soulless, purpose-built tower block apartment half a mile from the coast might be 'modern and efficient with wonderful views of the beach'.

Often when I've been writing some travel feature, I've tried to work out from a brochure the true cost of a certain holiday – adding on the supplements, taking away the discounts for children, etc., etc. I always end up phoning the holiday company for the answer. Invariably, they can't tell me immediately – they have to ring back because they can't work it out easily themselves. What hope is there for the ordinary holidaymaker?

Beating the brochures: To get the true picture, ask to look at a travel agent's copy of the *Agents' Hotel Gazetteer*. Most agencies have one under the counter and it has accurate and plain descriptions of the well used places. Hogg Robinson travel agencies have their own Fact Files – guides to resorts and hotels, with down-to-earth descriptions of places and accommodation. You can look at the Hogg Robinson guide for free at any of their branches.

Buying from travel agents: Travel agents earn their money from the commission they get from selling holidays and insurance policies. Unlike most shopkeepers, they don't buy their stock in advance. They order a holiday from a tour operator only when a customer has decided to buy one.

Tour operators spend their time and money persuading the travel agents to sell *their* packages rather than similar ones belonging to rival holiday companies. What this means nine times out of ten is that a travel agent won't be giving you unbiased advice.

Many agents have 'preferred' holiday companies they like to do business with – and who give them a higher commission for being on their 'preferred' list. Holiday companies also run incentive schemes for the sales clerks: if they sell so many holidays from one company to a certain country or resort that perhaps hasn't been selling too well, the clerk gets a colour TV or free air tickets or a shopping voucher.

So the right holiday for you at the price you want to pay may not be the one that an agent wants to sell you. Especially if they can earn more commission or a prize by selling you a different trip. I've heard of agents – in their eagerness to sell holidays, or is it their ignorance about holidays? – assuring clients that the Greek islands are 'famous for the food'. I suppose they are. Famous for not being among the great cuisines of the world. I've heard of people being told that The Gambia is 'just like the Canaries, only hotter'. Yes, and this book will win the Booker Prize. When I was a judge once for the 'Travel Counter Clerk of the Year' award, a *finalist* confidently said that San Antonio in Ibiza was quiet. Well, it is sort of quiet: for about two hours every day between dawn and breakfast. In short, for a variety of reasons, you shouldn't expect to get knowledgeable, unbiased advice from the first travel agent's you walk into.

Unless you get on very well with the people at one particular agency, you trust them and they truly know your likes and dislikes, *shop around*. You'll soon find out that some sales clerks are much better than others. Some are incapable of doing anything more than taking a booking, while others have a proven working knowledge of many holiday places or – even more important – if they don't know something about a company or a resort, they'll go to the trouble of finding out for you. Whatever sort of agent you end up using, you'll always be better off if you've already decided what kind of holiday you want, and you've done some homework.

Buying holidays direct: A fair number of holiday companies don't sell their holidays through a travel agent (which just proves that you can't get comprehensive advice from a travel agent). These companies, known in the business as 'direct sell' operators, deal with their customers by telephone, by post and sometimes face to face in their office.

Most of them organise their holidays in exactly the same way as the companies who use travel agents. But by cutting out the middleman (or middlewoman), they don't pay ten to fifteen per cent of the holiday price in commission. So that should mean cheaper holidays, shouldn't it? No. The direct sell companies do have to pay to advertise their holidays in newspapers and magazines and they have to bear the cost of posting out their brochures to any and every potential customer.

Find out about the direct sell companies from their advertisements in the weekend newspapers.

Who can you trust? Holiday companies don't go bankrupt or stop trading any more often than other sorts of companies. It just seems like it because, perhaps understandably, when a travel company does go bust and people are stranded abroad, or they lose all the money they paid for a trip they never get to take, it's a meaty story for the newspapers.

So how can you be sure that the company you book with

isn't likely to disappear in a puff of smoke? To be honest, you can't. The more important question is: how can you be sure that, if something does go wrong, you're going to be protected? Here's where the national organisations come in.

Four-letter words: ABTA: Most travel agencies and many holiday companies are members of the Association of British Travel Agents. If you book a holiday with an ABTA member who then ceases trading, you will be offered an alternative holiday or a full refund.

ATOL: All tour operators (including ABTA members) who sell holidays involving air travel on *charter* flights, or have charter-type arrangements on scheduled flights, have to hold an Air Tour Organiser's Licence. An ATOL is issued by the Civil Aviation Authority, the CAA, and in order to qualify for this licence they have to set up a financial bond which covers the costs of repaying and repatriating their customers if the company collapses.

If a holiday company that's *not* an ABTA member but does have an ATOL number stops trading, you will have your money refunded. If the company goes bust when you're on holiday, you will get home. However, unlike an ABTA member, an ATOL holder won't be able to offer you an alternative holiday. You'll need to find that yourself.

If you want to know if a travel agent or holiday company is a member of ABTA, just look for the sign. It's clearly displayed in the agents' shops and in the brochures. Spotting ATOL holders is a bit more difficult – thanks to some cowboy operators who have claimed to have an ATOL licence when they haven't. Their small print says that they are 'acting as agents for ATOL holders'. You might not be covered if they collapse. If you're in any doubt, you can check with the CAA whether a company is a genuine ATOL holder by phoning 071-379 7311.

Look for the bond: What about tour operators who don't belong to ABTA? After all, ABTA membership is not compulsory. ABTA travel agents only sell ABTA holidays but 'direct sell' companies don't use travel agents. And what about companies who sell holidays abroad but use only scheduled flights, or ferries and coaches? They don't need to be ATOL holders. Is it more risky to book a holiday with them?

Not necessarily. These companies might have arranged their own independent bonding system, to protect customers in the case of financial collapse. It will tell you in the brochure if they have.

There's an organisation called the Association of Independent Tour Operators (AITO). Their members are mostly small-scale travel companies who deal in 'specialist' holidays. The point is, AITO insist that all their member companies have some sort of bonding system to protect customers, so if you see AITO in the brochure, you're covered.

Ferry companies who sell package holidays belong to the Passenger Shipping Association (PSA). This organisation too has a bonding scheme for member companies, and again you should look for that guarantee in the brochure.

The Bus and Coach Council operates a similar bonding scheme to protect holidaymakers travelling on package tours with their member companies. Look for the symbol in the brochure.

You're on your own: So it shouldn't be too difficult to ensure that you're protected against a company going bust, whatever sort of holiday you buy. But if you choose to ignore all the above advice, and insist on booking with a company that has no recognised bonding system, heaven help you if they collapse. If you've already paid, you won't get your money back. If you're already abroad when it happens, you'll have to find your own way home, and pay for it. You have been warned.

Cover yourself: You can, of course, buy a travel insurance policy that covers you against the holiday company going bankrupt. If you think you need one, buy it as soon as you buy the holiday. Check, though, that the policy isn't one that only covers you for holiday companies that are bonded! Alternatively, you may be able to get your money back if you pay for your holiday with a credit card. You must pay the holiday *company* themselves, not a travel agent, and under the terms of the Consumer Credit Act the card company can be asked to reimburse you if the holiday cost more than £100. (This doesn't apply to charge cards or gold cards.) Don't expect a cheque by return of post. The credit card companies take their time and can need constant prodding.

Super savers – or are they? Whenever you're offered a 'bargain' holiday, check the cost of the extras you'll be paying. Does the price include airport taxes and all the travelling you'll have to do when you're abroad? Do you have to fly from an airport that's miles from your home? How much will *that* cost? And so on.

Don't expect a travel agent to lead you to the cheapest buys or to tell you about every special offer on the market. You need to be your own detective. Read the holiday advertisements in the newspapers (usually at the weekend) and in some magazines.

Some travel agents' special offers involve you buying the travel insurance policy that they sell. This is because they get a thirty-five to forty per cent commission on the travel policies they sell. If the offer tempts you but the insurance policy isn't exactly what you want, ask if you can buy a 'top up' to the policy to cover your particular requirements.

It's possible to get a discount or even a free place if you travel in a large group – usually of fifteen people or more.

Holidays cost less when you travel outside the most popular times. See **When to go**, page 5.

Travelling on weekdays can be cheaper than travelling at the weekends.

There are certain credit cards which run 'clubs' offering discount holidays (such as the Barclaycard Holiday Club, Trustcard Travel Club or Access Holiday Booking Service). You book your holiday by phone from the 'club', choosing from the brochures of the tour operators who are members of the scheme. Of course, you have to buy the holiday – or at least pay the deposit – with the appropriate credit card. The number of tour operators is limited (only fifty in Barclaycard's club, for instance), but the discounts apply to all the holidays in their brochures.

Foreign holidays for children under the age of two cost very little – often just £15 or perhaps ten per cent of the adult air fare. But the minute a child reaches two, holidays can cost as much as 90% of the adult holiday price.

Some brochures offer 'free' places for children – but these are often very limited in number, especially if the journey is by air. They're just an incentive to get you to book your holiday early, and they soon sell out. If you do manage to get a 'free' child place on an air holiday, you still usually have to pay the supplement for flying from a regional airport. You might also have to pay airport taxes.

If you're offered a self-catering bargain, you need to know the country's cost of living. A hotel holiday that's more expensive but includes meals could work out cheaper in the long run than self-catering. It probably would in the Caribbean.

Night flights are often cheaper than flying during the day – but work out what's involved. Flying back at night might not be such a bargain if you lose a day's work on your return because you're so tired.

Making the best of things After all that important advice about choosing the right package, I have to admit that whether you really enjoy your holiday or not depends on you and your attitude.

I have seen families at airports sticking out a long, long wait for a delayed plane and *having a good time*. I have seen other holidaymakers on a sugar-white tropical beach, by a swelegant, elegant hotel, scowling and whining because their cocktail is not cold enough.

In other words, there are people who can always make the most of a bad situation – 'We've bought a holiday to have a good time and we're damn well going to have a good time' – and people who will find fault whatever is offered them. Guess who's the happiest?

• Long-Stay Holidays

Spending the winter abroad is no longer just an option for the idle rich. There are some temptingly priced package holidays offering four weeks or more away from winter at home. The holiday companies claim that it's cheaper to spend the winter in Spain than to stay at home, and many retired people are finding that's true.

Obviously, you'll save on heating bills if you're not using your home through the winter. And if you stay away for a month or longer, with some careful forward planning, you can save money on other household expenses too.

Road tax: If you have a car at home, you can get a rebate on your Road Fund Licence for every calendar month your car is off the road. Ask for form V14 at a main post office. You send the completed form with your licence disc to the DVLC, Swansea SA99 1AL. It must be postmarked on or before the last day of the month before the month you want the rebate.

Once you've organised this, your licence is considered cancelled – not suspended. This means that when you come home you must re-tax your car before you can legally drive it again. Also, when it's not taxed you have to keep it off the public highway. It must be parked in a private drive or garage.

Car insurance: Most insurance companies will give a 'laid-up rebate' for a minimum of 28 days on your car insurance while it's off the road. They will, however, expect you to keep the car in a secure locked garage. Normally, your insurance is only partially suspended, leaving you with cover for fire and theft. It would be cheaper to suspend the whole policy but then you'd carry the cost if your car was stolen or vandalised when you were away.

Arrange for a cover note to be waiting for you when you get home so you can re-tax the car.

TV hire: If you hire a television and maybe a video, ask the company to suspend your contract while you're away. They should offer you the same make at the same rate when you return. If they won't do this for you, consider cancelling the contract (giving them the required notice) and finding a different company for when you come home.

Collecting your pension: If you have a book of orders which you cash each week at a post office, you can draw your retirement pension from any post office in the UK, but only up to two weeks unless you've made special arrangements. You *cannot* cash your orders while you are abroad. There are several alternatives:

- You can leave your pension to accumulate and cash it all when you get home. But you must cash each order within three months of the date on it, otherwise you have to return it to your local DSS to arrange a refund.
- You can arrange for the DSS to send your pension to you abroad. But it will only be sent every four weeks or thirteen weeks, and only in arrears. It will be sent in sterling by a payable order which you can cash locally. Write to the DSS at least a month before you go away to make the arrangements.
- You can arrange for your pension to be paid to some-one in the UK you nominate, and they can send money on to you. But again, it will only be paid to them every four or thirteen weeks and in arrears.
- If for some reason your husband or wife is not taking the holiday with you, he/she can collect your pension every week using your order book until it runs out. But then they won't be allowed to collect a new order book.

- Best of all is to organise for your pension to be paid into a bank or building society – if it isn't already. Allow four weeks for the change to be made. Then you can arrange for your bank to transfer money to a local bank where you are staying or post you a draft you can cash locally. You can ask a building society to pay regular sums of money direct to a bank and draw money while you're abroad through the bank. These arrangements are all best made in writing before you go away.

- However you choose to collect your pension, if you're planning to stay abroad *for more than three months* you have to tell the DSS.

Will your home be covered? Read the small print of your household insurance policy. Many policies automatically give only limited cover if your house is empty for 30 days or more. Contact your company and make special arrangements with them. They may charge you extra.

• DIY Packages

Don't knock the package holiday. Packages get millions of us to foreign places at prices we could never match if we set up the same holiday on our own. We individuals don't have the massive buying and negotiating power of the huge tour operators. And that's the crunch, of course. Not all of us want the holidays the tour operators put together. As we get more knowledgeable and confident about travelling abroad (probably thanks to those packages) we are more likely to want to set up our own holidays – even though an independent holiday can sometimes cost more than a similar packaged one.

Where to stay? Some lucky people own an apartment or a villa abroad. They've got no worries about accommodation: their only problem is how to get there as often as possible, and how to get there cheaply. Others 'own' a property for one or two weeks a year – a time-share. They too have been there before and know the ropes. (See pages 143–145 on the pros and cons of time-share.)

Some of us have friends or relatives who own a property abroad and are good enough to lend (or rent) it to us. We then just have to organise getting there. Mind you, before you agree to stay in someone else's place, even if it seems an offer too good to refuse, you should do some homework. Find out all you can about the place, what there is to do and see, how far it is from the airport and the shops – all the things you'd want to know before you booked a package holiday. Just because it's your friends' ideal holiday home, it may not suit you at all.

It's also possible to book accommodation abroad without it being part of a package deal. Some travel agents can book accommodation for holidays that aren't part of a package but more often you'll find this sort of holiday retreat in the small ads in newspapers and magazines. It's often self-catering accommodation, privately owned and possibly away from the popular tourist resorts.

Before you plump for an idyllic-sounding French farmhouse for two weeks, it's a good idea to find out something about the area. How easy is it to get to? Will you be stranded without a car? How are you going to get on if no one for miles around speaks English?

Taking pot luck: If you're carefree and optimistic – some might say foolhardy – you can always go abroad without having anywhere to stay at all, and take pot luck when you get there. Sometimes this can be a grave mistake. You'd be mad to turn up on the Spanish Costas in peak season and expect to stroll into a decent hotel which just happened to have a vacancy with a sea view. But if you're prepared to take a chance, in some places and at some times of the year you can find a bargain. You need to have a fairly happy-go-lucky attitude about where you stay, and it's not something I'd recommend if you're travelling with children.

Your best bet is in holiday areas, such as the Greek islands, where there is plenty of 'casual' accommodation – tavernas with tourist bedrooms, families who take in guests, etc. And the best time of the year is off-season. Basically, this means outside the school holiday periods. The locals are still keen to make a few bob from tourists, but their accommodation hasn't all been booked in advance. On some Greek islands, when you arrive on the ferry, you're met by a horde of landladies all clamouring to rent you a room. But always remember that in popular holiday places the best accommodation will have been booked in advance – probably by package tourists. You're being offered what's left.

If you want to stay in a proper hotel in a holiday resort, it is possible to find a room for yourself, without using a package tour. But what's the point? You'll never be able to negotiate the discount that the tour operators achieve by mass booking. Holidaymakers sometimes take a package and like the hotel they're booked into so much that before they go home they try to book the same room for themselves next year. They're amazed to find that the price the hotel quotes them is more than the whole of their package holiday.

When you're travelling independently and you want to book a hotel room, never be shy about asking to see the room before you agree to take it. In a quiet season, when the hotel is obviously not full, ask for a 'special price' – in other words, a discount. The later in the day it is, the better your chance of getting a price reduction. If you arrive early in the morning, the manager has the rest of the day to try to sell the room at full price. Around six at night is usually a good time – there's less likelihood of him finding another customer, and the hotel still has time to sell you a supper.

If you do find a hotel that suits you, and you'd like to return next year, take a note of the manager or owner's name and phone number. (If you have a room that you particularly like, make a note of the room number too.) Then you can book it yourself next year, as soon as you've fixed your holiday dates. But check the brochures first – they may be selling a holiday in the same hotel cheaper.

How to get there: Not so long ago, you could only buy cheap air tickets from what were called 'bucket shops'. Now cheapish air tickets to most popular places are available from tour operators and travel agents as well.

Shop around. That way, you'll discover the average going rate for the flights you want. (When you're quoted a price, find out whether the figure includes airport taxes.) Use the telephone for convenience or visit the travel agents in person – but avoid the busy shopping times at lunch hours and Saturdays. The clerks won't have the time to search for different prices for you.

If after a few calls or visits, it becomes obvious that the

flights you want on the dates you want are scarce, don't dither or you'll lose out. If you're offered a ticket but you still want to try some other places, ask to take an 'option' on it: the company holds the ticket for you a day or a few hours, without you being obliged to buy.

When a clerk in a travel agent's calls up information on a computer screen, it will only be selected information – it's biased towards the airlines who funded the computer programme. There is no one system that covers every airline. Another reason for shopping around.

Charter flights – when a tour operator has chartered a plane to fly customers on a specific package – are cheaper than full-fare tickets on an airline's scheduled flight to the same destination. Charter tickets are always returns, and you usually have to stay abroad for a set period of time – a week, 14 days or whatever. But charter tickets are only supposed to be sold as part of a package holiday. So if you only want to buy the flight, and not the accommodation, how do you take advantage of the cheaper charter fares?

To get round the regulations, when you buy a charter ticket on its own, the company gives you an accommodation voucher (or charges you a token £1 for it), so that in theory you're buying an 'inclusive' holiday – flights and accommodation. These vouchers will be for beds in campsites or in dormitories often miles away from the airport, in places that would never feature in any holiday brochure. The companies don't expect you to use this accommodation but, if you choose to try it, expect the absolute minimum in facilities. The company won't organise any transport to get you there from the airport.

You must take your accommodation voucher with you when you travel, even if you have no intention of using it. This is especially important when you're holidaying in Greece. The Greeks prefer independent travellers to fly on the (more expensive) scheduled airlines and can penalise charter passengers who have no evidence that they're using the charter flight as part of an inclusive holiday.

Don't miss your flight. A ticket for a charter flight is only valid on the day it's issued for. If you miss it you will have to throw yourself on the mercy of the airline and you will almost certainly forfeit your holiday.

Most years, flights to Athens, the smaller Greek islands and the Turkish coast – places popular with holidaymakers who don't have children – are heavily booked in September.

Ticket tips: You should avoid paying for an air ticket before you actually receive it. If you're asked to pay in full in advance, see if they will accept a reasonable deposit instead.

In travel talk jargon, a direct flight isn't the same as a non-stop flight. Direct flights can stop at airports on the way to your destination and may even involve changing planes. If you want to get somewhere without stopping midway, you must ask for a non-stop flight.

A full-fare airline ticket with a scheduled airline is valid for a year. You can change or cancel your booking up to the last minute, and even switch to a different airline on the same route. (For the problems this can cause, read on about overbooking.)

There are cheaper tickets for scheduled flights, with names like Apex, Super-Apex and so on. They are special excursion tickets and they suit most independent holidaymakers. You have to buy some at least two weeks, sometimes three weeks, in advance, and they're only valid for the dates printed on them. It's expensive to change these dates or cancel the ticket.

Children who are under two the day they fly out usually travel for a set price of around £15 and they don't get their own seat. They have to sit on your knee unless there happens to be an empty seat by you. On some flights there are reductions for children under twelve: the less popular the season, the higher the discounts for children.

Check your ticket: As soon as you have your ticket, phone the airline's reservation system. Give them the flight number and the date, and double-check that they have a confirmed reservation for you on that flight.

With a ticket for a scheduled flight (not a charter flight) look for the small box on the ticket marked 'status'. You need to see an 'OK' written in the box to know that your seat is confirmed.

Flying home: For a journey on a scheduled flight, telephone the local office of the airline within seventy-two hours of flying and confirm your booking with them. You need to do this because airlines often sell more tickets than there are seats on the plane. Astonishing but true. This is to allow for the passengers who don't turn up for the flight. If you have an unrestricted ticket you can change the day you fly without paying any penalty, and many travellers – usually business travellers – do just that. Result: some planes take off half-empty while others are overbooked.

The bumping game: Because of this cock-eyed system it's possible to turn up with a fully paid-for ticket for a scheduled flight and not be allowed on it because it's oversubscribed. Often it's the last passengers to check in who are 'bumped' off the flight. But in America a crazy sort of auction often breaks out.

In the US, the airline legally has to ask for volunteers who will wait for the next available flight – and has to compensate them. Waiting to see what the compensation will be for being 'bumped' has become a fine art among regular fliers around America.

Once when I was waiting for a short flight in the States, the steward announced that the flight was overbooked. He asked us for volunteers to wait for the next one, and said compensation would be so many dollars. No one moved. He tried again with a bigger compensation – and free return flights thrown in. Still no one stirred. Then he came up with an even higher figure, plus free return flights to Hawaii – first class. Twelve people rushed to the door. They knew the system and were playing the bumping game – waiting for what they judged to be the maximum compensation.

Elsewhere in the world there are minimum compensation scales laid down for people 'bumped' off planes who then arrive at their destination more than four to six hours later. However, some countries choose not to acknowledge these compensation scales! If you have a valid ticket to travel and you are 'bumped' you need to be very firm and persistent.

On one occasion I tried the 'I'm a journalist, I must be back in London with a very important story' routine. Another time I resorted to tears. Both eventually got me on the flight. If you can't persuade the airline to let you board, you must make them offer compensation on the spot.

● Holidays for the Single Traveller

If you're going on holiday by yourself, but you don't particularly want to spend all the time on your own, book a special interest holiday or a touring trip. On tours, from modest coach rides round the Lake District to sightseeing adventures round the Far East, the tour group nearly always has meals together, and what you do each day is organised for you.

On special interest holidays everyone has one passion in common, be it gardens, painting, bowls or whatever. This brings people together and means that you're not stuck for an opening conversation.

Paying extra for sleeping alone: It is grossly unfair on singles but if you want a hotel bedroom to yourself you often have to pay extra for the privilege. For some holidays the single room supplement can add over £100 to your final bill. The only alternative is to shop around until you find a hotel that waives this supplement. This can happen – but usually only in the off-peak seasons, so you have to be prepared to take your holiday then.

On touring holidays, some operators will try to match singles of the same sex who are willing to share a room with a stranger. You certainly won't be strangers at the end of the holiday.

It's often easier to team up for a friendly drink, a meal or an outing with a family you meet on holiday rather than with a couple. However, if you don't like the idea of being the lone single in a hotel full of children, avoid any holiday that advertises kiddies' clubs or low-price children's places.

Eating alone: Many restaurant managers resent the single diner because they spend only half the amount a couple would spend. These managers show their annoyance at you – the paying customer! – by plonking you on a neglected table by the kitchen or toilet and then, as soon as you've eaten, hustling you to pay up and move on.

If you don't like the table you're shown to, be assertive and point firmly to a different empty table and ask to sit there instead. If this fails for you, you can try this ruse at restaurants. Book a table for two. When you arrive, say that you'll wait for your friend at your (well placed) table. Make a pretend phone call and announce that – what a shame – you'll be dining alone after all.

- Don't be bullied into leaving quickly if you want to linger over your coffee. After all, you are paying the bill.
- Take a book to read between courses rather than stare self-consciously into space.
- If you fancy some wine and they don't serve half-bottles, ask for the cork and take your unfinished bottle away with you.

A broad abroad: A woman travelling abroad on her own doesn't have to be a young blonde in a miniskirt to suffer hassle from men. It's worse in some countries than others.

Wear a large wedding ring and invent a husband. If the 'husband' is 'away on army or police business', so much the better.

To avoid unwelcome visitors to your hotel room, don't flash around a room key that has your room number on it. If a waiter or barman asks for your room number when he's making out a bill, show him the key discreetly. Don't shout out the number for others to hear.

In all but the friendliest holiday hotels, it's easier for a man than a woman to strike up conversation with other men. Even though we are lurching towards the twenty-first century, a single woman's attempt to start a conversation with a male stranger can be misconstrued.

Buy a ticket for an evening excursion or to a show or the theatre. If all else fails and evenings become uncomfortable ordeals, change your daily routine. Go to bed early and get up early. Explore the local sights before breakfast. You'll get the best views for photographs – no tourists in the way – and you'll probably see far more of local life than when all the visitors are up and about.

• Honeymoon Hideaways

Never be shy when you're booking your honeymoon hotel. Make sure the travel agent, the tour company and the hotel know what you'll be celebrating. Some operators organise extras for honeymooners that don't appear on the bill, like flowers and a bottle of wine in the room. But they are wise to couples who try it on. Hoteliers and operators are tired of folk pretending they're newly wed in the hope of a free drink or meal. You might just be asked to show your marriage certificate before the goodies appear.

Double bed: If you want a double bed for your honeymoon – a reasonable expectation – you need to choose your country and your hotel carefully. In most tourist and business hotels a 'twin' room means two single beds and a 'double' should mean one large bed. But you'll be hard pressed to find a proper double bed in a Spanish hotel or in Greece. American hotels have wide, wide beds and even the two beds in their 'twin' rooms can each be nearly the size of a British standard double. In France, hold your arms out wide and ask for a *matrimonial*. Some countries call double beds 'French' beds.

Stuck with twin beds? If it's possible to push the twin beds together, put the mattresses *across* the beds and there'll be less chance of them sliding apart and one of you falling through the gap in the middle.

Wrong room: If you booked and were promised a double bed not a twin bedroom, and you're given the key to a twin room, complain at once. Don't wait until you've unpacked or until the next morning.

Passion-killers: If you're planning to honeymoon far far away, bear in mind that sugar-white beaches, tropical sunshine and film-star cocktails can take their toll on more than the joint savings account. Jet-lag, stomach bugs and sunburn are no respecters of romance.

GETTING MARRIED ABROAD

It is possible for two British citizens to marry abroad in a civil ceremony in certain countries – mainly glamorous-sounding tropical places like Antigua, Barbados, Jamaica, Bahamas, St Lucia, Hawaii and the Seychelles.

The ceremony usually takes place on a hotel beach or garden. It doesn't have to be in a registrar's or magistrate's office.

A few tour operators specialise in arranging the necessary paperwork and all the trimmings for a wedding at one of the holiday hotels – bridesmaids, best man, the cake and a photographer.

Some time before the trip you usually need to send the tour operator copies of your birth certificates (plus, where appropriate, proof of decree absolute for divorcees, a death certificate for widows and widowers, or proof if you've changed your name by deed poll), and if you are under twenty-one (or eighteen in the Seychelles) an affidavit stamped by the Notary Public that your parents have given their consent. Most places require you to be 'resident' for some days before the wedding.

How's this for romantic? One man arranged his tropical wedding this way but told his girlfriend only that they were going on holiday. He proposed on the plane. She said, 'Yes, but I haven't a thing to wear.' From his case he produced a wedding dress her girlfriend had secretly bought. I shudder to think what sort of holiday they'd have had if she'd said no.

Naming the day: These weddings are so popular that some hotels have been churning them out at a conveyor-belt rate of four or five a day. Most hotels now limit weddings to one a day at the most. But they're still very popular.

If you want to book the whole shebang through a specialist tour operator and stay in a hotel that organises these weddings, you need to plan your trip months in advance because of the long waiting list.

● Activity Holidays

Don't Just Lie There, Do Something

Some activity holidays and short breaks are a contrived excuse to fill empty hotel beds. The package cost of the accommodation plus the activity may be no less than the normal hotel price and the price of a session at the nearby sporting centre. In this case, you save money by booking the activity yourself and staying somewhere cheaper.

Special-interest tours and holidays are ideal for singles. You get to meet like-minded people – but you can be charged the dreaded single room supplement.

Dangerous deeds: Normal travel insurance policies don't cover you for 'dangerous' sports like scuba-diving or hang-gliding. Check the small print before you buy, and organise full insurance cover before you jump off or jump in.

Check that any instruction you are going to get is approved by the appropriate recognised authority. The Sports Council (16 Upper Woburn Place, London WC1H OQP, tel. 071–388 1277) will tell you which sporting authority to check with. (Send a stamped self-addressed envelope if you write to them.)

If your sporting activity includes lessons, before you book check that your instructor will speak good English.

• Skiing for Beginners

When the first intrepid Britishers tied planks of wood to their feet and slid down the snowy mountainsides of Europe, I doubt that they realised they were starting a multi-million-pound holiday industry.

As many winter holidaymakers now know, skiing isn't just for the rich and leisured classes. It's open to all of us who can afford the price of a winter package holiday and there's a whole range of companies offering to fly and bus us to the slopes.

Fans of the sport don't need me to offer any do's and don'ts. However, if you're considering buying your *first* skiing holiday, read on. And bear in mind that, whatever the brochures and travel features say, not everyone enjoys their time on the piste. Thousands of first-time skiers of all ages do come back, enthusing about the sport. For what it's worth, I hated every miserable, cold and painful minute of my first – and last – skiing trip.

Before you book: Find out exactly what your holiday price includes. As well as the journey and accommodation, first-time skiers need to budget for lessons and boot and ski hire. You'll also need special insurance (an ordinary holiday policy won't cover you) and possibly a lift pass. Some companies include a 'ski pack' in their holiday price which covers these expenses.

Find out how far you will have to travel every day to get to the slopes. Ideally, they should only be a walk away.

Steer clear of the purpose-built ski resorts if there's any

chance that after a day or two you won't like the sport. There will be very little else to do there. The Austrian resorts offer the most alternatives to skiing, which makes it the most suitable country for families where one of you isn't too keen on the art and needs something else to occupy themselves.

Ski clothes: If you can help it, don't buy specialist ski clothes for your first try – you might decide you never want to ski again. You can hire your boots where you hire your skis, and as for everything else, you can either borrow skiing gear or buy something that will double as everyday winter wear.

Don't wear denim jeans on the slopes. They shrink when they're wet and can freeze. If you can, borrow a padded pair of ski trousers or padded dungarees known as *salopettes* (which keep your midriff warmer). These won't get as soaked by wet snow.

- When you're buying or borrowing trousers, make sure you can touch your toes and squat down in them comfortably.
- If you don't already own an anorak, invest in a padded ski jacket that you won't feel embarrassed about wearing any time at home.
- Many layers of thin clothing keep you warmer than one thick sweater.
- You'll also need ski mittens or gloves (mittens are considered to be warmer).
- And you'll want a warm hat – preferably one that covers your ears.

Ski boots: Make absolutely certain that the ski boots you hire fit well and are comfortable. Don't be rushed into taking the first pair you're offered. Take them back and change them if you find they hurt your feet.

Anti-glare: You'll also need sunglasses or goggles to cut down the glare. Fix elastic or cord to the specs so you don't lose them if (when) you take a tumble. Plastic lenses are better than glass, which can shatter if you fall on them.

Without some protection for your eyes you can suffer from 'snow blindness' which makes eyes red and sore and will stop you skiing for a day or more.

Sun: Don't underestimate the strength of the sun at high altitudes. It's strong and intensified by the reflection from the snow. You'll need sunscreen and lip-salve. A jar of Vaseline is fine and cheap for keeping lips from chapping although it's too fiddly to apply on the slopes. Keep a jar in the bathroom for lips and very dry skin.

Après-ski: In most general holiday resorts evening dress is not glamorous – tracksuits or sweaters and warm cord trousers. You'll need strong footwear for walking around in the snow. If you don't have purpose-built snow boots, wellingtons – even when you wear them with thick socks – can make your feet feel very cold indeed.

Tipping: You're not expected to tip lift attendants and few British holidaymakers tip their ski instructor or their holiday rep. If you're staying in a 'chalet party' – where 'chalet' staff cook the meals – it's normal practice for the guests to take the cooks out for supper one evening. Don't worry, they'll let you know the form.

Ski tips

- You can pay for the hire of your boots and skis in advance – but then you're stuck with the hire shop that the holiday company uses.
- Be prepared for a mad rush on arrival as everyone queues to hire their skis and boots.
- Carry some mini-sized Mars bars for a mid-session pick-you-up on the slopes.
- Don't ski when you're tired. Many accidents happen towards the end of the afternoon and are caused by tiredness.

• Children's Activity Holidays

There are literally hundreds of companies offering activity holidays for children unaccompanied by their parents. Most of the holidays are in Britain. Accommodation is usually pretty basic and the big draw is all the different activities that children can try. Some holidays specialise in one main pursuit – football, perhaps, or computers. Others offer a range of sports and hobbies.

Anyone can open a children's holiday centre. There are no official requirements to meet. In fact the law makes it more difficult to start up a kennel for holidaying dogs. So you really do need to check out a place carefully before you send your children to it.

Before you book, ask the following questions. Don't book with any company that isn't happy to answer them and won't let you visit them for a look round when they are open.

- What qualifications and experience do the staff have?
- What is the ratio of staff to children, not counting any administration staff? One member of staff to every six kids is a good average. Remember that a sport like archery needs a higher degree of supervision than football or cricket.
- Does an adult sleep in the dormitory with the children, or at least next door to them?
- Are there any qualified resident medical staff and is there a doctor on call close by?
- Do the children ever have to leave the site? If, say, the riding stables or a river for canoeing is away from

the centre, how far is it and how do the children
have to get there?

- What happens on rainy days?
- Will the children need pocket money?
- Does the company offer insurance and what does it
  cover?
- Will there be any extras to pay?
- If the centre is in Britain, does the cost of the holiday
  include VAT?

• Holidays for the Disabled

People who have some disability have to do an unfair amount of homework to find a holiday that's going to work for them. Facilities in this country for disabled people can be pitifully poor. In many countries abroad, things are even worse.

Do your homework: Most of the associations that help people with special needs have some network of information about suitable holiday hotels. If you are in touch with any, ask them.

The Royal Association for Disability and Rehabilitation (RADAR) has a specialist holiday officer and a network of information on suitable hotels and tour operators. They also can offer information on activity and sporting holidays for the disabled. You can contact them direct or buy the two guides they publish – *Holidays in the British Isles* and *Holidays and Travel Abroad*. RADAR is at 25 Mortimer Street, London WIN 8AB, tel. 071–637 5400.

There's also a telephone travel agency that has RADAR's information on call. Telephone (0733) 558313.

The Holiday Care Service is a charity that compiles information useful to anyone with special holiday needs: people with mobility problems, the elderly, single-parent families, people on very low budgets, etc. They offer free and unbiased information – and plenty of it. You can telephone or write to them. Stamped addressed envelopes are appreciated. Donations are even better. Holiday Care Service, 2 Old Bank Chambers, Station Road, Horley, Surrey RH6 9HW, tel. (0293) 774535.

Finding a suitable holiday: Don't plan to travel on your own unless you are 110 per cent confident that you'll not need any sort of assistance from anyone during the journey and while you are away.

It helps to deal directly with the tour operator. Some companies have information about hotels that can accommodate holidaymakers with special needs. Very few travel agents seem to know this sort of thing. As you'll need to ask many questions before you book, you'll find it more reassuring to talk directly to the holiday company, not to gather all the information you need through a middle man. (A holiday company which isn't happy to spend time answering your queries shouldn't get your business. But don't expect a company that normally sells through a travel agent to offer you a discount because they're not paying an agent commission. They won't.)

Don't lie about your disability. You need to be completely honest and spell out exactly what you'll need and what you can and can't do for yourself.

Before you book, ask detailed questions. Be specific. For example, if you can't walk and you're told that you will be met at the airport and taken to your hotel, you need to ask about the transport. How, for example, will you climb into a coach?

If you have one major special request, perhaps for a bedroom on the ground floor and a hotel with no stairs, arrange to take an option on the holiday if you can, and reserve the right to book only when you have received a written promise that the company can and will provide what you need.

Consider the time of year you travel. In Europe, outside the peak summer months there are fewer crowds and cheaper prices.

Find out everything you possibly can about the area you plan to visit.

Plan your journey: Consider all the places and points along the way where you'll need help. You will have to organise this well in advance and then, a few days before you travel, contact the various people involved and check that they are ready and waiting for you.

Make sure you have full insurance cover. Some travel policies exclude holidaymakers with a disability or a pre-existing medical condition.

Find out whether you will need a medical certificate. An airline may insist on a certificate of fitness which your doctor will have to provide. You might also need a letter from your doctor before you can take out an insurance policy.

Make a check-list of any extra equipment you might need to take with you. (Don't expect to find a wheelchair repair kit or rubber sheets on sale in a holiday resort.)

Check whether any of your equipment will be classed as 'excess baggage'. Most airlines carry wheelchairs free of charge.

You might not need a wheelchair at home but will you be able to cope on holiday with the distances you might have to cover for sightseeing, shopping or going out to eat? If not, make the necessary arrangements for having a wheelchair well in advance.

Take more than a sufficient supply of all the medicines you might need. Take a written prescription for the medicines you use (with the dosage amounts clearly stated) in case of emergency.

Airlines and ferry companies will need to know your specific requirements.

You don't have to be registered as disabled to ask for free help at a British airport. If you have problems walking, you can ask for assistance. The airport should provide a wheelchair or an electric buggy and driver to get you through the airport and on to the plane. You need to tell the tour operator or the airline – and the airport – well in advance. It's as well also to phone them (or ask your travel agent to phone them) the day before the trip to check that you are expected. You may be asked to check in earlier than other passengers.

When Heathrow Airport announced in 1989 that porters were to charge a set £5 rate for helping passengers, they promised that other Heathrow staff would be on hand to help the disabled, the elderly and families with young children *for free*. The £5 porters wear red and grey uniforms. The Heathrow staff who should be there to help those of us struggling with children and other special needs wear blue – and they don't accept tips.

You will get the most help at airports during the quieter seasons. Saturdays in August are the busiest days of the year for travelling abroad.

The return journey is usually less smooth than your outward journey. During your holiday, remind the holiday rep about which day you are going home and ask her or him to check that the airport is ready to receive you.

• What to Take

But It's a Very Small Kitchen Sink . . .

What to take with you: There's a tried and tested rule about packing for a holiday: take half the clothes you think you'll need and twice the amount of money.

Think of holidays you've had in the past. I'll bet you've brought clothes home with you that you've never unpacked, let alone worn. However tempting it is to throw into the suitcase every item you like wearing, you simply have to be ruthless. Choose what you think could be the bare minimum of clothes you'll need. Spread them on the bed. Now put half the stuff back in the wardrobe.

You never run out of clothes on holiday – it's always the silly little things that you wish you'd remembered to pack. Regular travellers have one list of essentials which they refer to before every trip. If you make a list, don't throw it away when you get home: save it for your next holiday, with amendments and notes for improvements.

Divide your list into categories:

- Dressing up clothes
- Dressing down clothes, including beachwear
- Nightstuff
- Underwear
- Toiletries, medicines and suncreams
- Accessories like belts, jewellery
- Camera and film (see pages 134–139 on holiday photography)
- Entertainment: books, music, games, etc.

- Paperwork: tickets, passport, insurance, holiday money

Clothes for all occasions: To keep your baggage weight to a minimum, apply the double-up rule to the clothes you take. This decrees that most garments can serve two purposes. So a T-shirt, an underslip or a tracksuit can also become your nightwear. Flip-flops become bedroom slippers. A large sporty shirt can be a beach wrap and, if you need one, a dressing gown. A glitzy swimming costume for women worn under a skirt or trousers can double as a dressy top. A large thin square of fabric can work as a cover-up for burning shoulders on the beach and a cover-up for your head and bare arms in churches and mosques.

You need fewer clothes if you stick to items that colour co-ordinate.

When you can't decide which outfit to pack, remember that any outfit works if it looks good and *makes you feel good*.

Clothes in natural fibres such as cotton, silk and linen are cooler to wear in hot climates *but* however carefully you pack them they will crease. Synthetic fabrics are much less likely to crease but will make you stickier in the sun.

If you're going somewhere hot, you'll need a sunhat – but if it's a holiday resort you'll almost certainly be able to buy one there. If you have a favourite hat you want to take with you, it can be a nuisance to pack. The trick is to stuff the crown firmly with underwear and wrap T-shirts and jumpers round it to protect its shape in your suitcase. If everyone in your party is taking a hat, five packed together with one crown inside the other take up only a little more room than one hat. If you're taking two bikinis with you make sure they're the same shape – no funny white bits.

In the old days of the Grand Tour, a true Panama hat was made of such fine straw that a gentleman could fold it to fit his breast pocket. An elderly man at a very traditional London hat shop told me, with misty eyes, of Panamas so fine you could roll them and pull them through a wedding ring! Today, a properly foldable straw hat is a rare and costly find.

If you're heading for a cold climate, a hat's pretty useful there too. Your body loses about thirty per cent of its heat through the top of your head. Thin layers of different clothes keep you warmer in cold weather than one heavy sweater – and they're easier to pack. (It's the layers of air between the clothes that insulate you against the cold. That's why a good old-fashioned string vest is terrific in cold climates.)

If you think you're likely to get rained on, woollen fabrics dry out quicker than thick cotton. If you've ever been stuck with a pair of cold, wet denim jeans, you'll know what I mean. To protect you against a strong wind, a thin waterproof coat is as convenient as anything.

Toiletries and such: You don't need to empty the bathroom cabinet into your case for a week or two away. Your master-list of What To Pack should contain details of only the washing, shampooing and shaving stuff you *need*, not all the fancy things you think might come in handy. Plus anything that's appropriate to the sort of holiday you're taking. If you're going to be sweltering in a hot climate, for instance, take deodorant and/or talc, even if you don't generally use them. If you're going to be out in the cold, take a barrier cream or lip-salve.

However many items you take, to save space take them all in the smallest possible sizes. You're never going to use a large bottle of shampoo in two weeks, or a jumbo-size tube of toothpaste. During the year you should check out the chemists and cosmetic counters for special offers of sample-sized bottles and tubes and save them for your travel pack. In the case of small bottles, you can top them up from a large bottle before you go.

Always avoid glass containers: plastic is much safer. Anything that might leak (and where travelling's concerned, that means anything) should be wrapped separately in a plastic bag. Then when it splits open, you won't get shampoo all over your toothbrush.

Two – or even three – toilet bags are easier to pack than one large one. You can divide your toiletries into categories – hair, medicine, washing, shaving, etc. – and pack each group into a small wash pack or plastic bag.

Pack all the suntan creams and oils you think you'll need, unless you're sure you can buy your favourite brand at the place you're going. Wrap them all up in plastic bags, to avoid getting grease over everything. (More about suntanning on pages 129–133.)

Safety first: Pack a first-aid bag. A Rice Rule of Travel decrees that you will cut your hand, sprain your ankle and be badly stung twenty minutes after the only chemist's has closed for a long weekend.

You can buy most common medicaments in North American and European countries but you might find that they're more expensive than at home. They often have different names, too: there's a British travel sickness remedy called Kwells. In America, Kwell is a lotion for killing lice!

In your portable medicine-chest pack plasters, a small bandage, antiseptic cream, pain-killers, remedies for upset stomachs and constipation, anti-diarrhoea tablets and any medicines you use at home that you might need abroad. It's common to be affected by a change of temperature and atmosphere, so I pack sore throat lozenges and tablets for calming the symptoms of a head cold. (See pages 115–123 for more information about holiday health.)

Useful extras: Having insisted that you should pack the bare minimum, here are some handy items that you don't need, but which might make your holiday more enjoyable.

- You can never take too many plastic bags. They're invaluable for protecting leakable, breakable and dirty things. Dividing smaller items into groups – underwear, socks, toiletries, etc. – and stashing them in see-through bags makes for easier packing. (It also makes life easier for any customs officer who searches your bag.)
- For a tidier holiday bedroom, take a plastic shoe-tidy

– the sort that comes with transparent pockets and a
hook at the top. Pack the pockets with socks, smalls
and hankies; when you arrive, simply pull it out of
the case and hang it up. Or fill the pockets with
toiletries and hang it in the bathroom.

- Take a travelling iron if you really think you'll need
to wear well ironed clothes. But check that yours will
work on the voltage of your holiday country, and
pack an adaptor plug. The same goes for your travel
hair-dryer.

- If you want to take one of those Braun gas-driven
hair-stylers, you must pack it in the case that's going
to be checked in. They're not allowed in hand luggage – and the gas refills are not allowed on planes
at all, so fill up before you leave.

- If you can't live without a nice cup of tea, take some
tea-bags and a 'mini-boiler' – a heating element that
you put into a cup of water to boil it – or a travelling
jug that boils water. They save on room service bills.
A cup of herbal tea doesn't need milk. If you take a
heating element *don't* lay it on the bed. That's how
fatal hotel fires start.

- A small plastic bag filled with washing powder saves
on laundry bills.

- A tube of shoe polish – the sort with its own applic-
ator – smartens up shoes. As my grandmother used
to say, you can always judge a person by the state of
their shoes. Most posh hotel managers had grannies
who said the same thing.

- A folding Japanese-style paper fan will help you keep
your cool when the air-conditioning isn't up to
scratch.

- A thermos flask keeps hot drinks hot – and also keeps
cold drinks cold.

- A cool-bag keeps your refreshments fresh. You can
then buy drinks at supermarket prices and sip them
coolly on the beach – avoiding the more expensive
beach bar prices. The right size cool-bag can double
up as your travelling bag for hand luggage, and is

also useful for storing film for your camera (see pages 134–139 for photography hints).

- If you're going to be trudging round a strange city, a small compass will help you find your bearings when you get lost.
- Copy the addresses you'll need for postcards on to sticky labels and leave your address book at home.
- If you think you'll be buying any souvenir prints or posters, pack one of those long cardboard tubes to carry them home in uncrumpled.
- If you're taking presents abroad, don't gift-wrap them before you go. Security and customs officers may ask you to show what's inside. Wrap them if you like, but leave the sticky-taping and ribbon-tying until you arrive.

For self-catering holidays: The people you bought the holiday from should supply a list of what you need to take, but to be on the safe side, take your pick of the items listed above, and add:

- A sharp knife (but if you're flying, don't pack it in your hand luggage – it'll be confiscated).
- A bottle-opener which doubles as a corkscrew.
- Ice-cube bags and, if you're travelling with children, ice-lolly kits.
- Keep the door key to the property and the instructions on how to get there with you, not in your suitcase. If you're driving there, tie the key to the steering wheel.

Exotic holidays: More of us are travelling further afield than ever before – often to places that don't guarantee the same standards of comfort and hygiene that we expect in well established European resorts. Later in this book I'll be giving advice for particular far-flung countries, but here are some things it might be useful to take on your tropical trek.

- Insect repellent, and plenty of it.
- A mosquito plug – one of those plastic ball jobs which

you slip a fresh tablet into and plug into the electric socket every night. Never forget to plug it in at the first sign of dusk.

- A universal-size sink plug. If you can't get one, a squash ball can work as a sink plug.
- Air freshener if you're fastidious about drains and bathroom whiffs.
- Tissues and lavatory paper. Flatten toilet rolls before packing them.
- Presents for the locals. In many Third World countries, especially in Africa, children need pens for school. Pack some packets of standard ballpoint pens. (Never throw them at children from your car or coach. There have been cases of children being hit in the eye by a thoughtlessly thrown pen.) Postcards of our Royal Family or your home town can fascinate children – and their parents – in unsophisticated countries. Speaking of unsophisticated countries, Americans love Royal souvenirs too.

What you simply can't take: There are certain items that you must never take on aeroplanes – and a pretty bizarre list it is too!

Fireworks, flares and toy gun caps are banned, so are paints, thinners and firelighters, and also arsenic, cyanide and weedkiller. But if you can't enjoy a holiday without those items, you're reading the wrong book.

More important, you're not allowed to take hair sprays or any other aerosol in cans larger than half-litre. Lighter fuel is prohibited, both petrol and gas cylinders. You are allowed to carry safety matches but only as hand luggage.

Airport security officers will also confiscate 'harmless' fake items that could be mistaken for the real thing. Don't try to travel with toy guns or replicas. In the past, a certain aftershave has been confiscated because it was packaged in a plastic mock hand-grenade.

The cabin pressure in an aeroplane causes fountain pens to leak. The Parker Duofold Centennial fountain pen truly does not leak up in the air – but it costs more to buy than some foreign holidays. Carrying an ordinary fountain pen in an airtight single-cigar case can prevent it from leaking – or at least it will contain the mess. But you're better off not taking a fountain pen up aloft.

adapter plug   Wet wipes   Sunglasses

1. Loo Paper   HAT for Me

2. 'Coke' cool box

3. tea bags/coffee/choc

4. Washing powder.

5. plastic bags – dirty Washing

6. first aid Kit

7. travel iron

8. penknife – with Corkscrew

9. needle & cotton

• How To Take It With You

OK, so you've decided exactly what you want to take on holiday with you. Then you've realised that it was much too much, and you've put half of it back in the wardrobe. Then you've added a few more items that you forgot first time. Now how do you transport it?

What suitcase? You obviously want your case to be as damage-proof and theft-proof as possible. For my inside information on the most reliable sort of cases, I asked the airport baggage handlers. They're the men who load and unload the luggage and they're flinging suitcases around all day. They have neither the time nor the inclination to make sure your little soft-sided case of breakable bottles travels on the top of the pile. It's not their problem if it's buried under a ton of heavy luggage. It's not their problem, either, if a handle rips off when they give it a beefy pull. Based on the baggage handlers' experience here's the run-down on suitcases.

- Hard-sided suitcases with strengthened corners and one handle are the ones that withstand the roughest handling. The best bargain is a second-hand army-issue case. It has the recommended strong sides and reinforced corners that you get on very expensive cases.
- Recessed locks and handles that fold flat are better than those which stick out.
- If a case is locked, it's less likely to spring open accidentally.
- Handles should be strong and well-fitted. A weak one

will either snap off or tear out a section of the case. On a case with two handles, each one must be able to take the strain – you might always pick the thing up properly with both handles but a baggage handler will grab just one for pulling the case around.

- If you want a case with wheels on (a godsend if you have to traipse miles through airports with no trolleys), choose one with recessed wheels. Those that stick out can catch and break off.

- Don't overfill your case. The most common reason a case breaks is that too much has been packed into it.

- Tie a strap round your case. It makes for added security if it bursts open – and it also makes your case easier to spot on the luggage conveyor belt. I have counted fifteen identical cases on one carousel (black Delsey Club cases, by the way). If you don't use a strap, tie a ribbon round the handle for easier identification.

There's a thief about: There are occasions when a soft-sided case is more convenient than a solid, hard job. For instance, when you're doing your own loading, soft cases are easier to squash into cars and boats. But once you let it out of your sight, a soft case is less secure against thieves – it can easily be slit open with a knife.

A thief believes that the best pickings are in the smartest-looking, most expensive cases.

A case with a tongue and groove along the edge where it closes is almost impossible to prise open. A case which closes edge-to-edge can be forced open with much less effort.

Sharp-eyed burglars have been known to prowl around airports reading luggage labels. Why? It gives them addresses of people who are going to be away from home. The answer should be that you label your case on the outside with just your name and your destination (stick-on labels are more secure than tie-ons). However, as an extra security precaution against terrorism, some airlines are demanding that every case that's checked in must be labelled with the full name and address of the owner. If you're obliged to do this, tie on this label just before you hand over your case at the check-in desk.

Always stick a label on the *inside* of your case with your full name and address.

One, two or more? Carrying two medium-sized cases is better for your back than lugging one large one. (But most charter flights allow only one piece of checked-in luggage per passenger, so you can only take several cases if there's more than one of you travelling.) With two cases you can fill one with clothes and the other with awkward shaped items like shoes and toiletries. Alternatively, distribute the family's clothes around the different cases. Then, if one case goes missing *en route*, one person won't be without all their clothes. (See pages 53–54 for what to do about disappearing luggage.)

Babies under two don't have a baggage allowance but you can take a baby bag on board with supplies of nappies, food, etc. to see you through the journey. (See pages 103–111 about travelling with children.)

How to pack: *Traditional method:* Place shoes along the edge opposite the case handle. Pack the most creasable items flat on the bottom, with jumpers and underwear on top. The weight of the top layers stops the bottom layers from moving around and creasing. However, if you're taking a soft-sided case on a train or car journey, where you will always be in charge of storing it and it need never be underneath other luggage, put the lightest, most creasable items on top of the case.

The rolling method: This prevents hard creases forming and is particularly suitable for soft 'barrel' bags and casual holiday clothes. You don't fold your clothes, you *roll* each item. Lay them flat on the bed, checking that trouser creases and skirt pleats are arranged properly. Then roll them individually, loosely but firmly, round bottles and shoes – but only after packing anything leakable or dirty into plastic bags. Fit the rolls snugly together and distribute other hard items evenly round the clothes.

The concertina method: This avoids hard creases because the clothes are folded round each other. Start by laying a dress or a pair of trousers on the bottom of the case with the waistband against one end. What doesn't fit along the bottom, you leave hanging out of the opposite end of the case for now. Lay a second item on top but with the waistband against the other end of the case, and the part that doesn't fit hanging over the side opposite to the first overhang. OK, so far? The third item lies on top in the same direction as the first one. You can carry on in alternate directions with items like jackets, shirts and blouses, until you have several layers on the bottom of the case and leftovers hanging out at each end. Now pack soft, uncreasable things like underwear and socks on top of the layers, and fold the long clothes back into the case. Anything that's longer than twice the length of the case can be folded back over more soft items. This method is useful for packing smart, formal clothes in a suitcase. There will be no hard creases because nothing is folded straight back on to itself.

Whichever method you use, creases show up less if you turn clothes inside-out before packing. Jacket sleeves keep their shape better if you stuff them with undies, socks, or all those plastic bags you're taking. When you unpack at the other end, hanging a creased outfit in a steamy bathroom can help the creases to fall out.

Don't pack a suitcase as full as it will go. The Rice First Law of Packing says that clothes expand when they're away from home. Either that or suitcases shrink in hot climates. Whichever it is, when you come to pack for home, you invariably find that, mysteriously, it's more difficult to get everything in. And that's without any souvenirs you've bought to add to the load. So, when you're packing for departure, always leave a little room for growth.

Hand luggage: Each airline is allowed to make its own rules about how much you can carry with you on to a plane, and the captain has the final say on the matter.

You can always take one piece of luggage on board with you, as well as your handbag. (If you think this is unfair on men, well, there's no rule that says a man can't carry a handbag.) As a general rule this piece of luggage should not weigh more than 11lb. (5kg.) and you should be able to store it under your seat. Some airlines also insist that the length, depth and height of the bag added together should not come to more than forty-five inches.

It's up to you what you put into your hand luggage – but there are some general guidelines. *Don't* pack any essential paperwork in your main suitcase. Keep your tickets, your money, your passport and your insurance policy with you. Likewise, keep with you your spectacles and any medicine you have to take.

If you're going to a hot country, have some sun cream and insect repellant in your hand luggage. In some airports you can be bitten and burnt in the time between getting off the plane and collecting your main case.

If you carry essential toiletries, spare underwear, a T-shirt and a swimsuit in your hand luggage, then you can survive a day or two if the unthinkable happens and your suitcase goes astray.

When your case takes a holiday: There are few worse feelings than the one that hits your stomach when every case from the plane has appeared on the luggage carousel and been claimed by its owner – and yours isn't there.

Staring at the black hole of an empty chute won't magic it up. Instead you must report it missing and fill in a PIRF – Property Irregularity Report Form – *before* you leave the luggage hall. When you check in your luggage before your flight a baggage tag is stuck to your air ticket and it matches the one put on your case. You'll need to show this tag when the airline starts its hunt for your case. Show it but don't hand it over until you get your luggage back.

Generally speaking, airlines will offer some cash to help you get by without your luggage – *if you ask for it* – and you don't have to pay it back when your case turns up. However there is no standard legal rate and no legal obligation for this payment. Some insurance policies (see page 63) also entitle you to some cash after your case has been missing for a certain time, usually 12 hours. If your case never turns up, the airline will pay compensation but it is very little indeed – as low as US$9 per pound of weight – and bears no relation to the real worth of your holiday wardrobe.

If your case does appear on the carousel but it has been damaged or tampered with, again you must report it and complete a PIRF *before* you leave the airport, otherwise you jeopardise your claim for compensation.

I once rebelled against always lugging around hand luggage stuffed with necessities 'just in case'. I'd seen too many glamorous women swanning around airports with only a tiny elegant bag over their shoulder. I wanted to be like them, so I boarded my flight to the Caribbean carrying just a paperback book and a sweet little handbag. You've guessed it. I turned up in hot, sweaty Puerto Rico, in my London winter clothes – and my suitcase didn't.

I was travelling with a press group and our minder sprang into action for me. At one point I overheard her saying to a man in uniform, 'But you don't understand – she is a very important journalist.'

'Madame,' said the smarmy jerk, '*all* our passengers on British Airways are very important people.' He still didn't produce my case. It took 60 minutes of form-filling and shoulder-shrugging before I could crawl out of the airport. Then I discovered just how much a four-star hotel drugstore can charge for toothpaste and deodorant. I was also horrified to discover that I couldn't have accurately listed, described and valued everything I'd packed in my case.

I will say, however, that having no wardrobe gave me a sense of light-headed freedom. I didn't have to worry about how I dressed for dinner or meetings. I just made sure everyone knew my predicament. I was almost disappointed when two days later my case was delivered back to me from its illicit holiday in Antigua.

• Customs and Duty-Free

Being allowed to buy a limited amount of goods without paying duty or taxes on them has a historical origin. It dates back at least a hundred years, to the days when travelling between countries wasn't as easy as it is now, and refreshment *en route* was harder to come by – there weren't any motorway cafes, or restaurants on cross-channel ferries. To survive the long journeys, travellers had to take along their own food and drink (rather like fussy foodies feel they have to nowadays). If there was any left over at the end of the journey, they were allowed to keep it without paying customs duty on it.

Out of this has grown a multi-million-pound retail industry. The seven British airports in the BAA group (which don't include Luton and Manchester) alone account for twenty per cent of all the sales of perfume in this country. The duty- and tax-free shop at Heathrow's Terminal 2 has the fastest-moving stock of any shop in the world.

To most holidaymakers, buying duty-free is one of the perks of travelling – but sometimes it isn't a bargain at all.

Duty-free purchases are free of tax and duty – but never free of profit. Don't ever kid yourself that you're buying goods at cost price. One argument put forward for justifying their existence is that the profits the shops make help to subsidise the landing fees the airlines have to pay for using an airport. Without the shops, the fees would have to be increased and your holiday would cost more.

Buying as you leave: Check out your best high-street prices before you leave home. You'll find that some expensive items in the duty-free and tax-free shops can cost the same price or more.

When you're comparing alcohol prices, remember that many duty-free bottles (wine as well as spirits) are in litre or half-litre sizes. In shops at home they are usually only three-quarter-litre.

Ask yourself whether you're buying stuff because it will come in useful on holiday – or do you intend to bring it home with you? If so, is it really worth lugging those bottles and gifts around for a fortnight, just to save a few pounds?

If you want to take wine abroad, to drink in your room or on the beach, wineboxes are now available in most duty-free shops. It's a safer way of transporting plonk than bottles, and more convenient to use.

You won't save money by buying books at the airport – but you can buy the big-name best-sellers before the folks back home. In the bookshops in the departure lounges 'air-side' (once you are through passport control) you can buy books some weeks before they're officially published in Britain. You are in fact buying the export edition.

You might be tempted to buy your duty-free on the plane. Prices will be about the same – but you won't have the same choice. Storage space on planes is limited, so there's a smaller selection of brands on board to choose from.

Buying abroad: Airport shops in some countries abroad *don't* accept their local currency. Those are the countries that are hungry for 'hard currencies' and you can pay in sterling or dollars; they'll usually accept credit cards, too, and sometimes traveller's cheques.

The amount of stuff you can buy and bring into this country without paying duty on it varies according to where you buy it. There are two categories. You get a much bigger allowance on goods bought in European Community countries in ordinary shops, *not* in duty free areas. The second category, with a smaller allowance, includes goods bought in duty-free shops in EC countries, and any sort of shop anywhere else in the world. (The European Community countries are: Belgium, Denmark, France, Greece, Ireland, Italy, The Netherlands, Luxembourg, Portugal, Spain, the UK and West Germany.)

Beware of shopkeepers abroad – or sometimes even greedy holiday reps on commission – who insist that what you're buying isn't liable for tax or duty when you bring it home. If their advice differs from mine, and you don't know who to believe, just remember I'm not making any profit if you buy it.

These are the *current* allowances for the two groups, the maximum amounts you can bring into the UK without paying duty or tax:

1: Goods bought in the EC, but not in a duty-free shop (or ship or plane)

Alcohol
Either 1½ litres of spirits, plus 5 litres of wine
Or   3 litres of fortified wine, plus 5 litres of wine
Or   8 litres of wine
Plus   50 litres of beer

Tobacco
Either 300 cigarettes
Or   150 cigarillos
Or   75 cigars
Or   400 grammes of tobacco

Perfume: 75 grammes (85.5 ml. or 3 fl. oz.)
Toilet Water: 375cc (13 fl. oz.)

Any other goods: up to £250-worth (including your beer and a maximum of 25 lighters!)

2: Goods bought outside the EC, or any goods bought in a duty-free shop or on a ship or plane.

Alcohol
Either 1 litre of spirits, plus 2 litres of wine
Or   2 litres of fortified wine, plus 2 litres of wine
Or   4 litres of wine
Plus   50 litres of beer

Tobacco

Either 200 cigarettes
Or 100 cigarillos
Or 50 cigars
Or 250 grammes of tobacco

Perfume: 50 grammes (57 ml. or 2 fl. oz.)
Toilet Water: 250cc (8.5 fl. oz.)

Any other goods: £32–worth (including your beer and maximum 25 lighters)

All that's complicated enough – as most things to do with tax and duty are – but there are added complications in the small print.

For a start, your wine allowance only applies to still wines: sparkling wine counts as fortified wine. So does sherry, advocaat and most aperitifs – as long as they're not stronger than 22% alcohol (38.8 proof). 'Spirits' means anything stronger than that, and includes most liqueurs.

You can bring in your fifty litres of beer regardless of any other drinks, but its cost must be part of your 'other goods' allowance.

Nowadays, you don't have to buy all your allowed goods from within the same group. So you can, for example, buy your tobacco duty-free at the airport (using the smaller tobacco allowance) but your wine in an ordinary EC shop and claim the larger allowance for it. You can even buy your spirits in a duty-free shop (1 litre maximum) and your wine elsewhere in the EC (5 litres).

People under 17 are not entitled to any drinks or tobacco allowances.

Of course, you can legally bring in much more than your allowance – if you pay duty on the excess. But if you don't declare it you are committing a serious breach of the law, and there are people in uniform at every port and airport who can make life very unpleasant for you.

Old English customs

- Before you reach the customs desk, you should be

clear in your own mind whether or not you're 'over the limit' as regards allowable goods.

- If there are two or more of you going through customs together, your goods can be shared out between your luggage or all in one case – it's the total allowance that counts.
- If you know you're carrying more than you're allowed duty-free, you should go through the Red channel and declare it. If not, go through the Green channel – where you still might be spot-checked.
- Either way, a customs officer has the right to examine all of your luggage – and it's your responsibility to open it, unpack it and pack it up again afterwards. However annoying and inconvenient that might be, it never pays to get belligerent. Keep cool and remain polite.
- When a customs officer asks you, you must be able to list everything you've acquired on holiday. On the way home, make a list (with prices) of what you have bought or been given. Have this list ready to show the customs.
- If you're declaring your goods, pack them where you can easily find them to show.
- It's not true that an opened bottle of alcohol with a swig missing or a carton of cigarettes that isn't quite full don't count in the reckoning. They do.
- If you've taken something new and expensive – such as a new camera or leather coat – on holiday with you, you should also have taken along the receipt to prove that you bought it in Britain, and therefore you've already paid tax on it.

When Red is right: If you're bringing home shopping or gifts that amount to more than your allowance, declare them in the Red channel, show them if you're asked, and declare how much they're worth. You'll be charged VAT on them, plus import duty – which varies according to the sort of goods you're importing.

You can pay in cash (sterling, dollars or Irish pounds),

traveller's cheques (sterling or dollars) or with a personal cheque (covered by a bank card). You will be given a receipt, which you should keep. (And if you're taking any of your new purchases abroad with you in future, take this receipt with you, to prove that you've paid the tax.)

Don't try it on: If you're caught in the Green channel with more than your correct allowance you will be charged duty and tax *and* the goods will be confiscated. What's more, you can be fined on the spot or, if it's a serious offence, you'll be prosecuted and end up with a criminal record. In short, it just isn't worth it.

Don't pretend to be ignorant of the true cost of anything you've bought. In some countries, shopkeepers will happily give you two receipts for valuable items – one high one for insurance purposes, one low one for the customs. Don't try to kid the customs with one of these: they're wise to all the tricks – and they're surprisingly knowledgeable about the value of, for instance, Turkish carpets.

If you come through the Green channel unchallenged with more than your allowance, that's not necessarily the end of the matter. The customs and excise people have the right to search your home, confiscate goods and prosecute you long after your smuggling escapade.

• Insurance

Small Print? What Small Print . . . ?

There's no law that says you have to buy a special travel
insurance policy before you can leave the country. Many
people don't. They claim that they'll never need it and that
policies cost too much anyway. True, insurance isn't cheap
– but neither are air ambulances, emergency pain-killers or
the cost of replacing a stolen camera or a lost engagement
ring.

Can you be 100 per cent certain that your case won't go
astray, that your wallet won't get snitched or that a loony
cab-driver won't fling you over a cliff?

Which policy? Don't assume that the insurance policy recommended by your tour operator or your travel agent is
the right one for you. Use this chapter to decide exactly
what you want to be covered for, and don't buy a policy
unless it includes all your requirements. If your travel agent
claims that they can't sell you a policy that meets your
needs, you're free to buy one elsewhere.

When to buy: You can buy standard travel insurance policies at some British airports, but it really is best to organise
this bit of paperwork as soon as you've booked your trip.
Buy your travel insurance when you buy your holiday.
Then, if you've chosen the right policy, you won't lose
money if you have to cancel because of illness – yours or a
close relative's.

You can also be covered for cancelling because you're
made redundant, although it has to be a job loss that quali-
fies as a redundancy under government legislation (so if you

lose a job you've only had for six months you won't be covered).

Some policies will reimburse you if you have to cancel because you're summoned for jury service or because your home or office is burgled or damaged and the police need you in Britain.

Medical cover: You'll obviously want to be covered for any medical treatment you have to pay for abroad. But for complete peace of mind, you should choose a policy that also includes an emergency flight home if you need it – in an 'air ambulance' if necessary.

If you're ill or injured you might need to fly home early to get treatment not available abroad. A scheduled air ticket bought on the spot always costs an awful lot more than a holiday charter ticket. And if, heaven forbid, you're on a stretcher you won't be able to sit on an ordinary airline seat. You'll need to buy three or four seats, and possibly pay for a nurse and/or doctor to fly home with you. You can see how the bills mount up.

It's not true that in America you have to re-mortgage your house when you sneeze. However, hospital treatment – or even just going to the doctor – is horrendously expensive in the States and the insurance cover provided by your policy should reflect this.

An 'air ambulance' flight home from Miami costs £25,000 – and that doesn't include the bill for medication and hospital treatment. So, for trips to America and Canada, medical insurance cover of £1,000,000 per person is not too high.

For Europe, where an air ambulance flight home costs £4000 just from Northern France, you should have medical cover of £250,000 and for the rest of the world, £500,000.

Free medical treatment?: It is possible to get treatment free or at a reduced cost from countries which have health care arrangements with the UK. (Leaflet SA40 from your local Department of Health office explains the details.) But don't rely only on these arrangements because the cover provided under the different national health schemes is not always comprehensive and it *never* covers the cost of being brought home.

Emergency phone number: Choose a policy that offers an emergency telephone number which is manned twenty-four hours a day. An emergency telephone number that only works during office hours is no good to someone run over by a coach on Saturday morning.

What's your camera worth? Check a policy's single-article limit. A maximum of £200 for each item that's lost or stolen may sound generous – but will that cover your camera, your video camera or your engagement ring? If not, you can 'top up' some policies to cover articles worth more than the normal limit.

Your home policy You probably already have a policy that covers your household contents. You might find it also covers your personal belongings when you take them with you abroad. Check this out. But, of course, you'll still need medical insurance.

Activity holidays: You need special cover if you're planning to have a go at any potentially dangerous sports. This can mean skiing, water-skiing, scuba-diving, parascending and so on. Ordinary travel policies have exclusion clauses about being injured while indulging on a risky activity.

Delays: You can insure against a delayed departure. This doesn't mean that you won't suffer any delays, only that if you do you can claim some money. A meagre £30 or so won't make up for spending twelve hours of your precious holiday in an airport lounge, but it's better than nothing.

Baggage delays: You can also buy a policy that pays you money to cover emergency shopping if your baggage is delayed for more than 12 hours on the journey out. You can usually only claim this once you are back home and, of course, you'll need written proof that your bag was delayed. Keep a copy of the PIRF form you filled in at the airport (see missing luggage on page 53).

Free insurance: Sometimes travel agents offer free

insurance when you buy a holiday from them. Charge cards and credit cards can also offer free insurance when you buy airline tickets using their card. If you find yourself entitled to free insurance, check that the policy does cover everything you might need. If it doesn't, offer to pay for a 'top up' that adds the cover you want.

Claiming: When something gets lost or stolen, you have to make a report to the local police within twenty-four hours and then show written evidence that you did (a copy of the report) to the insurance company as soon as you get home. Yes, in countries like Spain this can involve tedious queueing and hours waiting in a police station out of the sun. But without the police paperwork you can't make an insurance claim.

If the friendly local bobby refuses to fill out a form (which can happen) take his name and/or number, the address of the station where you tried to make a report and then ask your hotel manager or tour rep to make and sign a statement about your loss. Give all these details to the insurance company.

When you're claiming for a lost or delayed suitcase, you need to show a copy of the PIRF form you filled in at the airport (see page 53).

What the small print really means: Just because you've bought an insurance policy, that doesn't mean that money automatically appears when things go wrong. If you leave the family jewels unguarded on the beach while you go for a swim, the insurers can refuse to pay up. They'll say you weren't paying 'reasonable care and attention'.

Likewise if, after a cocktail or six, you dance your way through closed glass doors, you can find your claim for medical expenses refused because you were well 'under the influence of alcohol or drugs'.

A true story: three men on holiday in Italy befriended a local girl. They went off to the beach for the day, leaving their valuables locked in her car boot. When she disappeared, their cameras, clothes, passports and cash disappeared with her. They claimed on their insurance – but didn't get a penny. The insurers insisted that entrusting everything to a stranger was not 'paying due care and attention'.

False claims: Some people so begrudge paying for insurance that, when they have reason to make a claim, they exaggerate it for all they're worth. Holiday reps call it the 'gold chain syndrome'. Somebody has their handbag snatched and their claim form claims that in this designer leather handbag (funny how plastic bags never get snatched) was not only the wallet but also, surprise surprise, a valuable gold chain.

I asked some holiday reps what they do in these cases. 'Let's just say', they said, 'that when it comes to helping the client organise new traveller's cheques and police reports we are not as helpful as we could be.'

Take your policy with you: Always travel with a copy of your insurance policy to hand – not stowed in your suitcase. You never know when you might need it.

Being ever the pessimist, when I'm travelling alone I let someone in the place I'm visiting know about my policy and its emergency telephone number. Hopefully, if I'm out for the count, someone will know to summon the financial help.

To know more: For more information you can contact the Association of British Insurers. They represent 430 insurance companies and are obviously in the business of encouraging people to buy insurance, but they do advise on special problems with buying or claiming on insurance. They also give out a free leaflet on holiday insurance. Send a stamped self-addressed envelope to the Association of British Insurers, Aldermary House, Queen Street, London EC4N 1TT.

And if it rains? No. You can't insure against bad weather on holiday. 'Loss of enjoyment', it seems, isn't a recognisable claim in the insurance world.

• Holiday Money

How to take it with you: Probably the best way to take money abroad is to take a mixture: some sterling, some foreign cash, one or more credit cards and some traveller's cheques and/or Eurocheques or Postcheques.

Don't automatically buy foreign currency and traveller's cheques from your local bank. You can also buy them from post offices (through Girobank) and from some building societies – which often charge a low commission or none at all.

Cash: It is useful to have some local cash when you arrive. You might need it to get to your accommodation and for tipping porters. You'll also need something to tide you over if you arrive after the banks have closed for a weekend or a bank holiday.

It's not worth buying a lot of foreign money in Britain, unless you're travelling to a country with a strong currency, like Germany, Japan or Switzerland, when you might get a better exchange rate here. For countries with weaker economies – Portugal, Greece, Turkey, Yugoslavia and, to some extent, Spain – you'll get a better rate of exchange once you are there.

The major foreign banks have branches in Britain – most of them in the City of London or the West End. If you live or work near one of these, you'll find for instance that you get more pesetas for your money from a Spanish bank than from your regular high-street bank.

It's not always easy to buy certain foreign currencies in

Britain, but most foreign airports have a money-changing kiosk so you can change some cash as soon as you arrive.

Always ask for small denominations. You know what a bus conductor says in Britain if you offer him a £10 note. Abroad, they say the same, only louder.

The black market: If you're in a country where there is an established black market for 'hard' currencies like our pound and the American dollar, use your common sense. If a stranger sidles up to you in the street and offers you a black-market rate of exchange (which is always much higher than the official rate) for your sterling, you ought to walk away. If you don't and he cheats you, you've no comeback. If he delivers the goods but you're being watched by an undercover policemen, you're in trouble.

However, in a few countries – Bulgaria for instance – black-market currency deals are so common as to be almost normal. If you're tempted, take advice from someone who knows the score, like your holiday rep. If you do dabble in the black market, you must also change some money officially and keep the receipts. You may be asked to show them when you leave the country.

Changing money abroad

- You can't change coins – including pound coins – only notes.
- Many foreign countries don't recognise Scottish or Irish notes.
- When you're comparing exchange rates between banks, hotels and money-changing agencies, allow for commission charges. A money-changer advertising favourable rates will be hiding a chunky commission charge.
- Your hotel might change money at a worse rate than the bank – but calculate whether the journey to the bank, with the safety risk involved as you'll be carrying your cash and passport, and the possible bank queues, are worth the difference.

Losing cash: The obvious drawback to carrying cash –

sterling and foreign – is losing it. A travel insurance policy should cover you if you lose up to £250 but you forfeit the first £20 and you need a written police report before you can make your claim. You must report the loss to the local police within twenty-four hours and make sure they give you an official report. If, as has been known to happen, they won't hand over some slip of paper acknowledging your report, ask the holiday rep to write you one. The insurance company won't replace the money straight away. You'll only get their cheque when you're back home and some time after you've made the claim.

Traveller's cheques: Traveller's cheques are popular because they are simple to use, are replaceable if you lose them and are heavily advertised. You do, however, have to pay for them in full when you first get them and not when you spend them. You can cash unspent ones back home.

When you get your cheques you sign each one once, and then you sign it a second time as you spend them. Never add the second signature until you are in front of the cashier or the shop assistant who is taking the cheque.

You must always keep the slip with your cheque numbers separate from your cheques. If your cheques go missing while you're away, you can get them replaced (as long as you have a record of their numbers) within two or three working days – sometimes faster.

You can buy traveller's cheques in some foreign currencies, although they can cost more. Buy cheques in small denominations for countries that don't allow the export of their currency (and give lousy exchange rates for changing it back to sterling).

In Austria, Belgium, Italy, Malta, Holland and Scandinavian countries you're charged a commission on the *number* of cheques you cash, rather than on the amount you change, so for these countries take cheques for large amounts.

Always take *dollar* traveller's cheques to the USA. You can spend them like cash in shops, hotels and restaurants. No one, including banks, wants to know about sterling cheques.

Flashing the plastic: The use of credit and charge cards is spreading. In America they consider you a non-person if you don't have any. (The first time I went to America I had no plastic and a hotel refused to let me book in. Showing them my treasured British passport and a wodge of traveller's cheques cut no ice. To have any sort of nice day over there you have to flash the plastic to show that you are a person worthy of credit.)

- Check the expiry date of your card(s). You need them to be valid during the whole of your holiday.
- If you lose a card you must report it to the company right away or you can be responsible for any charges the thief runs up using your card. So take the office number of the card company with you.
- When you use a credit card to pay a bill abroad, you pay in the local currency and it's billed to your account back home. It is converted into sterling at the rate that is in existence on the day the bill hits the UK.
- You can arrange to have a higher spending limit on a credit card just for the weeks you're away. Write to the card company some weeks before your holiday and ask them to organise it.
- You can use the cards to get cash from a bank but you pay a commission for it.

Bargaining with plastic In countries like Turkey and Morocco where you have to haggle and negotiate a price when you're shopping, you'll find that, even when you've agreed the 'final' price, if you then try to pay with plastic, the price goes back up ten per cent or so. Paying with cash gets you the better price.

'Proper' retailers – shopkeepers, restaurant owners and hoteliers, etc. – are not supposed to charge you extra for using a credit card. If anyone does try to charge you extra for paying with plastic, you should threaten to report them to the card company. If that cuts no ice and you pay the extra, keep the receipt and report them once you get home. Stallholders in markets, kasbahs and souks will say they're offering a 'discount for cash' rather than charging commission for using the card. In countries with a black market for valued foreign currency you'll get an even bigger discount if you pay in sterling cash.

Eurocheques: Eurocheques work like ordinary cheques but, unlike normal cheques, you can use them throughout Europe – including the Eastern bloc (though it's not so easy in the USSR) – and some North African countries, too. When you want to pay with a Eurocheque, you write out the amount in the foreign currency.

Unlike traveller's cheques, your money is not tied up in advance – although, if your Eurocheques go missing on holiday, you can't get them replaced while you are still abroad.

You pay £5 a year for a Eurocheque guarantee card and then pay a commission to the foreign bank on the amounts you cash, plus 30p a cheque to your bank at home. A Eurocheque Card can sometimes draw cash from a machine. As well as drawing cash from banks, you can use the cheques in shops and restaurants which belong to the Eurocheque scheme.

The guarantee card covers each cheque up to a sum of around £100 (depending on the currency) and there's no limit to the number of cheques you can use to pay one bill.

Retailers are not supposed to charge you extra for using Eurocheques. However, when I used one once in a supermarket in Boulogne, the bill was bumped up 10%. (I regret that I frostily paid up because I'd spent ages choosing my trolley-load of wines and cheese and the ferry was due to leave any minute . . .)

Girobank Postcheques: If you have an account with Girobank you can buy Postcheques which come with a free Postcheque card. You use them to withdraw cash from post offices in thirty-two European countries.

Postcheques cost £5 for a book of ten, and you're charged a commission which is debited from your account back home along with the amounts you withdraw. The big advantage, as well as not having your money tied up in advance, is that post offices keep longer hours than banks and are usually open on Saturdays.

Electronic cash: Season by season, banking technology becomes more computerised and more international. Gradually countries are joining up with systems that allow card-holders to use hole-in-the-wall cash dispensers abroad. The systems are still patchy and you should check with your bank and credit card and charge card companies for the latest news on whether and where you can use your cards.

If you can't memorise your private PIN number (your personal number that activates your card) you should write it down somewhere – but in disguise. Perhaps as part of a pretend telephone number.

Keep a note – separate from your wallet – of the telephone number of your local bank and the number of your account, in case you need to telephone them for emergency funds.

Coming home

- Towards the end of your holiday, change only small amounts – you don't want to be stuck with a load of foreign money that you'll have to change back, paying a commission every time.
- In countries with strict rules about how much local currency you can import and export, you must keep the receipts when you change money. At the end of your trip you won't be allowed to change any money back into sterling without these receipts. (The receipts show that you didn't smuggle the stuff in or change money on the black market.)
- Keep all your receipts and vouchers from your holiday so that when you're back home you can accurately check your credit card statements and, with Eurocheques or Postcheques, your bank statements.
- Don't bring foreign coins home, except as souvenirs. You won't be able to change them into sterling, though some British charities will take them as gifts.

- Also avoid bringing home foreign notes of high value. You often get a poorer exchange rate on high-value notes.
- Don't forget to keep some sterling for getting you home once you land back in Britain.

• Paperwork for Drivers

As soon as you plan to take your car abroad, your list of paperwork to organise before you leave home gets longer.

You need to have a full driving licence. You'll also need to travel with the car's original vehicle registration document (log book). And you would be foolhardy not to travel with special motoring insurance.

If you're taking a car abroad that's not yours, you will need a registration certificate VE103. If you've hired the car, the hire company will supply it. If it's a leased car, the leasing company will provide it if you tell them you're going abroad. And if you've simply borrowed a car, get the certificate from the AA.

Insurance for drivers: Start organising your foreign motor insurance at least a month before you plan to drive off. Contact your insurance company or the AA or RAC.

Your normal fully comprehensive policy is not 'fully comp' once you're abroad. It only covers you for the minimum legal requirement of the country you're driving in.

You can buy a Green Card which, in effect, tops up your normal policy to give you fully comprehensive cover abroad. In most European Community countries, you don't legally need to have one, but it makes sense to get one before you leave home. (Although Greece is a member of the EC, for the time being a Green Card is still compulsory there.)

Find out whether your insurance company will count any claims made abroad against your home no-claims bonus. Some do. Some don't.

Spain: If you're planning to drive in Spain you should also get a Bail Bond. If you're involved in a traffic accident in Spain, you can find your car and property impounded – and possibly you, too – even if the accident wasn't your fault.

A Bail Bond is a financial guarantee that your insurance company will pay up if you are held responsible for the accident. It won't prevent nasty accidents happening but it will prevent you spending part of your holiday behind the wrong sort of Spanish bars.

Also in Spain, the conventional green UK driving licence is not officially recognised unless it's accompanied by a translation stamped by a Spanish Consulate. Alternatively, you can get an International Driving Permit from the AA, which is recognised everywhere in Europe. The new-style pink UK licence *is* recognised in Spain – but you can't change your green licence for a pink one just for the sake of driving abroad.

Ireland: If you're going to drive in the Irish Republic, check whether your normal motoring policy covers you. Some do. Some don't.

Hiring a car abroad: If you are thinking of hiring a car when you are away you'll need to take your driving licence with you, and so will anyone who might want to take their turn at the wheel. It has to be a full licence, not a provisional one. Full insurance cover should be provided by the hire company.

In most European countries you have to be twenty-one or over before you can hire a car. In Portugal the minimum is twenty-three, and in Italy and Malta it's twenty-five.

(See also the information about preparing your car on pages 91–95 and requirements for individual countries on pages 146–228.)

• Passport

Bureaucracy Rules, OK?

If you won on the premium bonds today, you might just want to say, 'To hell with work and the weather, first thing tomorrow morning let's whizz off down the Nile, or go and see the Taj Mahal or say hello to Mickey in Disneyland.' But with all the prize money in the world you wouldn't be able to. Not unless you happened to already own a full current passport and the proper visa.

Holidays abroad are exciting but they do involve some tedious bits of organising before you can get there. Skimp the paperwork at your peril.

Passports: Only your bank balance stops you from buying a holiday to just about anywhere in the world. But no country will let you in if you don't have a current passport. If you're a British citizen there are two sorts of passport you can buy.

- The 'full' passport lasts for ten years, is only available from passport offices and currently costs £15 (or £22.50 for husband and wife on the same passport).
- The British Visitor's Passport lasts for one year, is available from main post offices and currently costs £7.50 (or £11.25 for husband and wife on the same passport).
- You can travel to most Western European countries (plus Canada, Bermuda and Turkey) with just a British Visitor's Passport, and stay there for a maximum of three months. Everywhere else wants to see a full ten-year passport before they will allow you in.

- If you're a British citizen you don't need a passport to visit the Irish Republic, the Channel Islands or the Isle of Man.
- The point about husband and wife being on the same passport is that only one of them can travel alone. If the husband is the actual passport-holder, say, and the wife is included, he can use the passport by himself, but she can't use it unless she's travelling with him.
- Circumstances change, so always check out the latest situation once you've booked your trip. If you hold a current British Visitor's Passport, or plan to get one, just check with your travel agent or tour operator that you don't need a full passport for your trip.
- If you already have a passport, check that it's not out of date and that it won't expire during your holiday.

How to get one: The British Visitor's Passport is easy to acquire – provided you don't mind queueing in post offices. All you need is two passport photographs – the sort you buy in a photo booth. Fill in the form they give you at a main post office, hand over £7.50, and you've got a passport.

If you need a full ten-year passport, you have to apply for it at a passport office. They're in Belfast, Glasgow, Liverpool, London, Newport (Gwent) and Peterborough. You don't need to apply in person, you can do it by post, but either way, you probably won't get it straight away. In the busy periods in late spring and summer you might have to wait weeks for one – so plan early.

You need a completed application form (pick them up at a main post office) and two photos – again pictures from a photo booth are fine. One picture has to be signed by a 'suitable' British subject who has known you for at least two years. 'Suitable' is supposed to mean an MP, JP, clergyman, lawyer, bank manager, policeman, doctor or similar. Actually, I've never heard of anyone's application being turned down because of an 'unsuitable' signature. It seems that anyone who can do joined-up writing will do.

Saving time: You don't have to apply to the passport office nearest to where you live. The London office has a history of appalling backlogs, and some of the others have ground to a halt through industrial disputes in recent years. If you need a full passport in a hurry, and you suspect that the office nearest you is going to keep you waiting, it's worth phoning round all the others to try to find one that can help you quickly.

The delays at all of them are longest in the late spring and summer, and, if you apply in person, that's when the queues are longest. Take a good book.

Children

- Children under eight can't have their own British Visitor's Passport.
- But children of any age can hold a ten-year passport. David Frost applied for his first-born's passport the week the child arrived.
- However, most ordinary mortals are content just to add children to their own passports – that is, the passport of a parent, step-parent, adoptive parent or brother or sister, but not grandparent.
- A parent can use the passport without travelling with the child named on it, but the child can't travel without the parent.
- Children have to have their own passports when they are sixteen.

Vaccination certificates: You sometimes need to show vaccination certificates when you enter a country. It's a good idea to take them with you anyway, and the safest place is in your passport. These certificates usually come in a booklet, which you can fix to the passport's spine with an elastic band.

Remember . . . Wise travellers memorise their passport number, the date it was issued and where it was issued.

You're asked for this information on the immigration forms you fill in when you arrive at a country. You sometimes also need it when you fill in a registration form at a hotel, and also when you want to change money. Memorise the details and you needn't keep fumbling around for your precious passport. These three facts would come in very useful if you ever lost your passport. And knowing them off by heart doesn't half impress other passengers!

Visas: Having a full ten-year passport isn't enough to get you into some countries. You also need a visa. You usually have to buy this from the country's embassy in London before your trip. It's their way of vetting who visits them and usually charging you for the privilege. The visa is usually a stamp on a page of your passport.

Your travel agent or tour operator should tell you if you need a visa and can probably organise getting one for you.

Applying personally to an embassy for a visa is only feasible if you work or live in London. Embassies are only open on weekdays for visa applications, and some keep short opening hours. They all close on our national holidays – and on theirs. To apply by post, allow at least four to six weeks (although travel agents might have a courier system which cuts down the time).

You need to have a passport *before* you can apply for a visa. Some countries insist that existing passports have at least six months left to run.

If you apply by post, photocopy all the paperwork you send and include a strong, large, self-addressed stamped envelope. Send it all by registered mail. You may also have to send a postal order to cover the fee, as many embassies won't take cheques, and certainly not credit cards.

The price of forgetfulness: If you turn up at an airport or ferry port without a passport, and you're travelling to a country that accepts British Visitor's Passports, you might have time to find a photo booth and a post office *and* catch your connection.

If you need a visa for where you're going and you turn up at the airport without it, you'll probably not be allowed to board the plane. If you do get on the plane, it's very unlikely that you'll be allowed into the country when you arrive. Most countries will keep you at the airport until they can put you on the first available flight home.

• Setting Off

The first day of a holiday is one of the most stressful days of the year. The combination of excitement, anxiety, schedules and simple fear of the unknown often result in the worst family rows since . . . well, the same day last year.

The journey, I find, is never totally stress-free, but you can eliminate some of the worries by a bit of forward planning.

Be informed: Well before you leave, tune into the news bulletins and road traffic reports. This is the one day of the year when a hijack, a multiple motorway pile-up, a seaman's strike, fog or a city-centre protest march will directly affect you and your journey plans.

Timing: Work out a conservative estimate for your journey time to the ferry port, station or airport, allowing for refreshment stops, roadworks, bad weather and heavy holiday traffic. To save tempers and stress on all but the shortest journeys, add an hour to your estimate.

Just in case: Leave a contact number, address, or at least your planned route with a friend or relative. In dire emergencies where you are not easily contactable, the *Daily Mail* will print emergency messages in their overseas editions. Contact them direct or through the AA.

Give the burglars a holiday: Ask a neighbour regularly to tidy up unwanted papers from your front door. You can avoid telling the world that you're away by cancelling your newspaper and milk deliveries. But this doesn't prevent junk mail and free newspapers from being stuffed into your letter box and piled up on your doorstep.

This same neighbour might perhaps also be persuaded to mow your normally neat front lawn, thus stopping a sharp-eyed burglar being offered another clue that you're away.

- Pay any outstanding bills, especially any 'red' final ones, before you leave.
- If you're going away in the depths of winter, and you fear burst pipes, reset the central heating timer so that it comes on for a few hours between midnight and dawn – the coldest time.
- Otherwise, turn off the gas and water at the mains.
- Any house plants that aren't going to be watered for two weeks will survive better in a cool room. Or you can stand pots in a few inches of water in the bath.
- Invest in a time switch into which you can plug a light and a radio. Set it to come on at various times to give the illusion that the house is occupied.

OK, you've done all that and no one has lost their temper yet. Now you're ready for the journey.

• Plane Sailing

It's not just people with a fear of flying who are under stress when they travel anywhere by plane. All passengers at airports have one thing in common – some form of anxiety. Show me a completely relaxed, laid-back adult passenger and I'll show you someone about to miss a plane. Or a drunk.

The right ticket? Long before you get to the airport, there are things to worry about. Tour companies are quick off the mark when it comes to chasing your money but not so speedy at sending out your tickets. Start seriously nagging them if they haven't arrived two weeks before departure.

When you have the tickets in your hand never assume that they will be correct. I learned my lesson one eve of departure, when a friend casually glanced at my ticket and pointed out that the flight had taken off ten hours ago. I'd been issued with a ticket for the wrong date.

Thankfully on this occasion it was possible to sort out the tour operator's mistake in time – but the trip could so easily have ended in tears at Gatwick. I feel sick just thinking about it. So read and re-read your tickets, hotel vouchers and all the information sent with them. Check the dates and times of the flights, and your check-in time.

Getting to the airport: Do you need to drive to the airport? The two busiest in Britain, Gatwick and Heathrow, prefer passengers to arrive by public transport or taxi. They know that people in cars often arrive late because of the sheer weight of traffic on the nearby roads and the all too frequent roadworks.

Some time before your holiday, check out the different ways to get to the airport you're travelling from, the time each method takes, and the cost.

If you're travelling alone or as a couple, ask your travel agent if there's another couple or single booked for a flight from the same airport at a similar time. If there is, you could arrange to share one taxi, which can work out as cheap per person as public transport. And more convenient.

If you do decide to drive to the airport, remember that finding the long-term car-park, organising parking and getting back to the departure lounge can take as long as forty minutes, so allow for that.

Keep your car-park ticket with your wallet, tickets and passport. Your holiday suntan will soon fade if you have to go through the rigmarole of claiming your car without a ticket. You can be asked to pay a hefty penalty too.

Of course, drivers shouldn't drink alcohol on the flight home.

Which terminal? If you're flying from Heathrow or Gatwick, check which terminal you leave from. There are four at Heathrow and two at Gatwick – and they're miles apart. Turning up at the wrong one costs a lot in time and effort.

Airport attitudes: Airport planners have told me that passengers behave in two predictable ways when they're under stress at an airport. Either they become unnaturally belligerent, loud and angry – the 'Don't talk to me about delays, miss, I know my rights!' brigade. Or they become unnaturally meek and obedient and lose the ability to think for themselves. If someone tells them to join an obviously wrong queue and stay there, they will do it unquestioningly. Which sort are you?

The same planners also told me that what most groups of people under stress need for reassurance is eye contact with each other. That's why chairs in airport waiting areas are often fixed in straight rows – so that you *can't* easily make eye contact with your family or friends. Why? Because if you want chairs in a circle or opposite each other, you have to sit in the restaurants and cafés. And to sit there you have to spend money. Nice one, eh?

On arrival: As soon as you arrive at the airport, search out your check-in desk. This isn't always straightforward because the airline you're flying with may well use another airline's desk.

Your check-in time is stated on your ticket or with accompanying instructions. (If in doubt, ask your travel agent or the airline.) The latest check-in time can be as much as two hours before your flight is due to take off.

Airlines like you to check in in plenty of time. If everyone checked in at the last possible minute the plane couldn't keep to its schedule. The people who run the airports *love* you to check in early. The sooner you're inside, the more time you have to spend money at the airport.

On holiday flights, most passengers form a queue before the check-in desk opens. But it's impossible to predict just when the queues are going to be longest. If you turn up close to the final check-in time, you might find that you have the desk to yourself because everyone's already checked in – or there can be hundreds of them still waiting. If you turn up really early, you might be first in line – or you might find that hundreds of people have arrived even earlier.

Whenever you plan to reach the check-in desk, you have to be prepared for a tedious wait. I have learnt the importance of patience, tolerance and relaxing deep breathing exercises!

If you're travelling in a group, you don't all necessarily have to queue for checking in. Nip to the head of the queue to ask whether one person can check in for you all. If that's OK, the poor soul who is 'volunteered' has to have all the luggage that's being checked in, and all your passports and tickets. With today's tighter security measures, the airline may insist (quite reasonably) that the owner of every suitcase and/or every ticket should present themselves in person before being allocated a seat on the plane.

Checking in: At the check-in desk, you hand over your ticket and all your bags and cases except what you're taking on board as hand luggage. You may be asked to show your passport, especially if you're visiting a country that demands you have a visa.

The clerk allocates you a seat and gives you a boarding card showing your seat number. He/she labels your luggage and sticks a corresponding luggage label tag on your ticket.

Check-in choices: You'll be asked whether you want to sit in a smoking or no smoking section of the plane. Unless you're one of the last to book in you should also have a choice of aisle or window seat. If you're not offered a choice, a friendly request usually works if the seats are available. Pompous demands rarely do.

On a long flight, where you sit is important. If you like to walk around whenever you can, or you have a weak bladder, an aisle seat is better than a window seat. You usually have a better view of the movie screen from an aisle seat. If four of you want to sit together it's easier to talk to each other if two sit either side of an aisle in the same row. Two behind two is trickier for conversation.

If you want to get your head down for a good doze, a window seat is best. You have the wall at the side to rest on and you won't be disturbed by neighbours climbing over you to get to the loo. Middle seats are the worst – unless you are a small child or you're very fond of the people either side of you.

Plane designs differ. Asking for the seat number you once had on a flight you've enjoyed won't necessarily produce the same position on a different flight.

If you've made arrangements in advance for a cot or for a vegetarian meal (which are not always available on charter flights) it should show up on the check-in computer. Remind the clerk anyway. In some foreign countries – particularly less sophisticated places with a more primitive booking system – when you check in to fly home, you will be faced with a complete denial that any special order ever existed. Having something in writing on official paper can magic up your request. But not always.

Check again: Don't leave the check-in desk without making sure you've been given a boarding card, the return part of your ticket, and a luggage label tag for each case you checked in. With a scheduled airline ticket, the part of the ticket belonging to this flight will be torn off and tucked into your boarding card. You'll need to surrender this at the gate before you get on the flight. (I never thought this was important until I lost my ticket slip in the departure lounge. I had a boarding card but without the voucher I wasn't going to be allowed on the flight. By sheer chance I spotted it on the floor under the chair I'd been waiting on. Phew! They let me on.)

Now you can relax – or try to. Once you've got a boarding card and your luggage is being loaded on to the plane, *it's impossible to miss your flight*. Why? Well, the airlines won't thank me for mentioning this, but these days a plane simply won't take off until everyone who has checked in luggage is on board. For security reasons, they refuse to fly with luggage that isn't accompanied by its rightful owner. So they won't go without you.

Of course, if you relax so much now that you're late arriving at the departure gate and you keep the plane waiting, you won't be terribly popular with the staff and your fellow passengers. Don't hold me responsible for the treatment you get on board.

IN THE AIR

The change of pressure during take-off and landing can painfully affect your ears, especially if you're suffering from a head cold. It helps to chew gum, suck a sweet or make yourself keep yawning.

Once the plane is airborne and the seat belt sign is switched off, most cabin crews are happy to let you change seats. If you spot an empty row of seats, move there as soon as you can and you have a ready-made bed (although only in planes that don't have fixed armrests).

I once travelled with an off-duty stewardess and saw her counting seats as we took off. I asked her why and she explained that she always memorised how many rows there were between her seat and the nearest emergency door.

Then, in the very unlikely event of having to evacuate the plane in thick smoke, or if the lights failed, she could count her way to the exit in the dark.

If you want to sleep in your seat, always fasten your seat belt so that if there's turbulence you won't be woken up and told to fasten it. If you don't want to be woken for meals and drinks, tell the stewardess or pin a note saying so to your headrest or lapel.

Flight fitness: On all but the shortest journeys your body can suffer from the pressure in the cabin, from the dry air-conditioned atmosphere and from being immobile for so long. If you want to arrive in good physical shape, follow these tips:

- Take some exercise. When the seat belt sign is off and the crew aren't serving meals, take a walk up and down the plane.
- Sitting in your seat, tense up every muscle in your body (don't forget your neck) and then relax. Do this six times every half-hour.
- Keeping your ankles still, move your feet in circles ten times clockwise and ten times anti-clockwise.
- Altitude makes your feet swell, so don't wear tight shoes. Some people swear by brown paper bags – honestly – and wear one on each foot during a flight. If you can't bring yourself to try that, just rest your feet on your in-flight luggage in front of you. The higher your feet are off the floor, the less they'll swell.
- The extra potassium you get in tomatoes and bananas may also help prevent puffy ankles. Eat them before the flight.
- If stress or fear of flying causes hyperventilation – exaggerated uncontrolled breathing attacks – breathe into a paper bag. (There should be one in the seat pocket in front of you.)
- On-board air-conditioning can be chilly. Have a sweater and socks handy.
- The air on board has a drying effect on skin. Lash

on the moisturiser and hand cream. Drying skin causes tans to fade fast.

- If you wear contact lenses, make sure you have your wetting solution with you.
- If you plan to take a pill to help you sleep during the flight, don't swallow it until you are airborne. You'll be very groggy if the flight is delayed, and you need to be alert for news of its rescheduled time.

Eating and drinking aloft: Most in-flight meals include meat – which puts a strain on the digestive system, on top of everything else your body's going through. On scheduled flights, you can order vegetarian meals, but you must do this at least two days before the flight.

Some airlines come up trumps with well thought-out, individually prepared vegetarian feasts. Others offer you the same as everyone else's meal but without the meat. On one flight when I tried this, Swissair's pre-packed main meal for meat-eaters included a half-bottle of red wine. Vegetarians got a bottle of mineral water!

There are no rules to stop you from taking your own snacks on board. Healthy, fresh *hard* fruit is excellent. Soft fruit bruises and ripens too easily.

The effect of alcohol is accelerated by the pressure in the cabin. If you drink alcohol, take equal amounts of water or juice. Some airlines object to you taking your own booze to drink on board (they want you to buy theirs). Be discreet if you do. Plastic bottles are best. You can leave them in the magazine pocket to be cleared by the cleaners after the flight.

Inconveniences: The queue for the toilets is longest after meals and after the movie finishes. On long journeys it's also lengthy before breakfast (all that shaving and teeth-cleaning going on) and forty minutes before landing. The state of the toilets on all but the best-run airlines deteriorates during the journey.

When you land: There's no point in fighting to get off the plane first unless you're travelling independently with hand luggage only. If you've got a case in the hold, you're at the mercy of the baggage handlers, so you may as well stay in your seat. Even if you're last off the plane, you'll still reach the baggage retrieval area before your case does. And if you're on a package tour, you won't leave the airport until the last people on your bus have collected their cases.

For quick getaways and to be first in the queue at immigration (and first for a trolley) remember that if you have to board a bus to get from the plane to the airport building, the last on the bus is the first off.

Jet-lag: There's no miracle cure pill for jet-lag. If you fly east or west through different time-zones your body has to adjust to the sudden time change. You are told it's lunch-time but your body thinks it's the middle of the night and acts accordingly.

The most canny and experienced travellers I know all suffer from some effects of jet-lag – usually sleeping and eating patterns up the creek. I live a very unregulated life. My nine-to-five day can as easily be six-to-three or ten-to-midnight. Yet my body clock can never properly cope with a major time change. Among other things, jet-lag makes me weepy.

The best advice is to *think* yourself into the time-zone you're going to. For example, if you're flying to Florida and it's dawn *there* when you're leaving home, as you approach the airport start telling your body and your brain that it's dawn *now*. On the flight, try to eat and sleep accordingly – go to sleep when they're going to bed in Florida. When it's breakfast time in Florida, clean your teeth and have some sort of breakfast. By the time you arrive, your body might just be in tune with Florida time.

Even so, you should never make any important decisions the day after a long flight, even if you think you feel OK. Don't change a lot of money. Don't buy holiday excursions. Don't tackle a long drive.

- The effects of jet-lag are usually increased by alcohol. The more you drink, the less chance you are giving your body to adapt.

- If you want to force your body to sleep, by all means take a mild sleeping pill – but not before the plane takes off.
- If you need to stay awake to chime in with the new time-zone, coffee and tea are harmless stimulants. They work best if you've given them up for a few days beforehand.
- Jet-lag can affect a woman's menstrual cycle. Take tampons and painkillers (if you use them), even if you're not expecting a period during your stay.
- The homeopathic remedy to help alleviate jet-lag symptoms is arnica.

Clothes for the journey: If you're flying somewhere hot during the British winter, travel to the airport in your winter coat but leave it in the left luggage or locked in the boot of your car. (Ring the airport first to check that there is a left luggage and that it will be open.) Otherwise, don't wear a coat – it'll be a cumbersome nuisance at the other end.

- Wear layers of clothing that you can strip off as the temperature hots up. Then you can use each layer on its own on holiday.
- Dress for comfort and dress for a dirty journey – white clothes somehow never stay white.
- Don't wear a tight waistband. Your middle will expand as you sit for hours in a plane.
- Natural fabrics like cotton, linen and wool are the most efficient at keeping you cool or warm. Unfortunately, they also crease the most.

• Journeys by Car

What's the French for Fan Belt?

Service: Have your car and tyres checked and serviced a week or two before you leave – to give you or the garage time to put right any faults. Make sure the garage knows the sort of distances you are about to tackle. Tyre pressures should be increased to compensate for a weighty load and fast long-haul driving.

Beam me up: For driving abroad you have to make your headlights dip the other way. Do this by fitting headlamp converters which are mask sheets of PVC or with clip-on lens beam deflectors. You can't use the beam deflectors on halogen lamps.

Reset the angle of your headlights to compensate for the load you're carrying. Otherwise, come nightfall, you'll find yourself with just a view of the treetops.

Wings: Fix a near-side (left) wing mirror if your car doesn't already have one. You will need it when you are driving on the right.

Spare tyre: Check the spare a week before you leave. This gives you time to replace, repair or inflate it. Sadly, cars aren't designed for easy access to the spare when a car boot is loaded.

Test the jack before you leave. Test that your wheel brace really can unlock and tighten up the wheel nuts.

Fluids: Have new brake fluid put in if you are going to have to tackle hills and mountains. Take some spare transmission fluid if you're driving an automatic. It's not easily available abroad.

Spares: Take some spares with you. What you take depends on your car, where you're taking it and for how long. You can hire a kit of spares from the AA. As well as suitable spares, the AA recommend you also take:

- a pair of windscreen wiper blades
- a torch
- a length of electrical cable
- a fire extinguisher
- an inner tube of the correct type for your tyres
- a tow rope
- a roll of insulating or adhesive tape
- your car manufacturer's handbook.

Engine oil is often sold only in large cans abroad. If you might need some for a small top-up take your own bottle.

If you'll be travelling in remote areas and you're worried about running out of fuel, take an empty can and fill it up with petrol once you get abroad – you're not allowed to take a can of petrol on a ferry. (However, travelling with a spare can of petrol in the car is illegal in Greece, Italy and Portugal.)

Check that the boot locks properly and easily. If it doesn't, oil it.

Check that your maps are up to date. If not, you could miss out on the latest stretches of motorways and bypasses. Larger libraries stock road maps that you can borrow, although not always the newest versions.

Packing the car

- To avoid tempers and delays, have an advance rehearsal. Pack the car with empty cases to check that all your luggage fits in.
- Take the tool kit out of the boot. Put it back in, only after you've loaded up. Then it'll be to hand if you need it.
- Use soft bags, uncrushable towels and jumpers as

wedges between the main cases to stop them rattling and shifting.

- Never block the rear window or pack anything round the driver's legs.
- Pack all the paperwork, passports, insurance, tickets, accommodation vouchers, etc. in a file or plastic bag and stow it under the driver's seat. (Check the paperwork you need for driving abroad on pages 73–74.)
- Inside the car, pack tissues (which you can use as lavatory paper in public loos where it's always missing), a roll of plastic bags for rubbish, refresher tissues and a wet cloth and a wet leather in plastic bags for cleaning the windscreen.
- If there's the remotest chance that one of you will be car sick, pack a towel, wet flannel, extra plastic bags, air freshener, peppermints and bottled still water.
- Pack a first-aid kit and put it in an easily accessible place. A soft bag is easier to stow than a tin.
- A collection of small bags is easier to pack than one large one. Pack food in one bag, drinks in another, in-car entertainments in another, freshening-up stuff in yet another.

Roof-racks: Avoid roof-racks if possible. You'll have to unload them for overnight stops where there is no secure private parking. A roof rack increases petrol consumption more than pulling a trailer does. (However, you have to pay extra to take a trailer on a ferry, but not a roof-rack.)

If you do use a roof-rack, load it with the lightest objects – picnic chairs, lilos and other inflatables, and push-chairs. This keeps the extra petrol consumption as low as possible. The more top-heavy a car, the more petrol you use.

Put each suitcase on the rack in a heavy-duty polythene bag – the sort you find on farms or at builder's merchants. (Use clean ones, of course.) These are waterproof and stronger than dustbin liners which rip in the wind. Strap everything down as firmly as possible.

Skis on roof racks should be loaded with their tips pointed to the rear of the car.

Weight-watchers: Don't overload your car. It is dangerous because the car won't handle properly. You're liable to be stopped and booked and not allowed to drive on until you have somehow reduced the weight. In some countries, overloading can also mean on-the-spot fines. Overloading your car affects your insurance cover. Your car handbook will tell you the maximum weight you can carry. If in doubt, weigh your luggage on the bathroom scales.

No phones: If you have a car phone, remove it before you leave home. It could be confiscated by Continental customs officials because of the interference they cause to the emergency radio frequencies abroad. If you forget before you leave home, the AA will look after your car phone at their port office – for a fee.

For the journey: Have your maps and any directions you've been given to hand in the front of the car. A highlighter pen is the best way to mark a route. Keep a torch handy for reading at night.

Have warm cover-up clothes accessible in the car for a chilly night, the ferry decks and any mountain passes *en route*.

Pack an overnight bag (or two) and load them last – with the tool bag – to make them easily accessible.

After a long drive in hot weather, your windscreen will be plastered with dead insects. A damp newspaper is good for getting the worst of the carnage off.

If you're going to a self-catering holiday flat or cottage, have to hand everything you'll need as soon as you arrive – torch, tea-bags, milk, bottle opener . . . If you have the key to your accommodation, tie it to the steering wheel or somewhere equally conspicuous.

It's different abroad: Know the legal requirements and local driving laws in the country/countries you're visiting.

- You must display a GB sticker on the rear of your car. Ferry companies and motoring organisations supply them.
- A warning triangle is compulsory in most European

countries – if you have to stop you place it on the road behind you to warn oncoming traffic.

- By law in Spain and Yugoslavia you must carry a set of headlamp replacement bulbs.
- A fire extinguisher is compulsory if you're driving in Greece.
- In Greece, Austria and Yugoslavia you must by law have a first-aid kit in the car.
- Always have your licence, the vehicle registration document and your insurance cover with you. You will be fined on the spot if you can't show them. Police abroad can – and do – make random spot-checks on motorists.

Keep right: Fix a note or a reminder ribbon to the steering wheel, your seat belt, the dashboard or your ignition key, reminding you to drive on the right.

The dangerous moment is not, as you might think, the first fifty kilometres. Here you are concentrating hard. You're probably keeping down your speed and you are in a steam of other careful GBs from the ferry. The danger point comes when you are relaxed and pretty confident. You stop for petrol or a coffee on a quiet country road – and when you drive off, there's little to remind you to drive on the right, so from habit you automatically pull out to the left.

Oops! If you're unlucky enough to be involved in an accident, take photographs to show the vehicles involved, their registration plates and the positions they are in. They will act as a reminder when it comes to the form-filling. Your priority is obviously to help anyone injured and to avoid further accidents by warning oncoming traffic (use the triangular warning sign).

Police make spot-checks for speeding at motorway toll gates. They can tell by the time and distance of your journey recorded on the ticket whether you have been speeding. If you have, you will be fined on the spot.

Homeward bound: For customs on the journey home, have

a list of all your buys and duty-frees to hand. Pack your shopping in an accessible place for the customs officers to inspect. If they choose to search your car, the more stream-lined the packing, the faster and easier the search. The customs people are under no obligation to help you repack the car.

Remember to take off your headlamp converters for the journey home this side of the water.

Car hire: If you plan to take a hired car abroad you must tell the hire company and get special documentation. See page 73.

When you're hiring a car abroad, you can save the cost of two days' hire if your accommodation is a shortish dis-tance from the airport. Use taxis between your accommo-dation and the airport on the first and last days of the holiday. (Hire cars are charged on a twenty-four-hour basis.)

Give your hire car a thorough once-over before you drive it away. Check the headlights, the spare tyre, the wheel brace, the jack and the locks. Ask for a test drive and check the brakes.

When you first hire the car, don't sign a statement declar-ing that it's in good working order and free from any defect. At the most you will only have test-driven it for five minutes. If you are asked to sign, cross out the clause and write something like 'No apparent defects on inspection. Appears to be working normally'.

Don't sign a blank credit or charge card voucher when you collect the car. Pay the deposit in traveller's cheques or cash if you can. If you need to pay by credit or charge card, fill in the estimated total hire charge before you sign. If the total is different when you come to settle up, sign a new voucher and tear up every coupon of the old voucher – theirs as well as yours. If you sign a blank voucher and you then have a dispute with the company (if the car breaks down, say, but they insist on charging you the full rental) you will have to go through the long and boring rigmarole of claiming back what is owed you through the card company.

Read the insurance policy carefully. You must declare the names (and show the licences) of everyone who will be driving the car when it's in your charge. If someone who has not been named has an accident when they're at the wheel, they – and you as passenger – will not be covered by the insurance. If they are stopped by the police when they are driving they will soon discover that they are committing the criminal offence of driving without insurance.

If you need to put oil in a hired car, keep the receipt and claim it back.

Pulling a caravan

- Make a list of the caravan's contents to show the customs at frontiers.
- Check that your direction indicator lights flash at the regulation 60–129 flashes a minute. Most don't once they're connected to a caravan or trailer and you will need to fix a special heavy-duty unit or a relay device.
- Caravans – and boats and trailers – must have a unique chassis number for identification if they're taken abroad. If yours hasn't, you can buy an identification plate from the AA.
- The way you pack a caravan affects the way it tows. Put heavy items over the axle, not at the front or back of the caravan. Heavier items should be on or near the floor.
- A loaded caravan should never weigh more than eighty-five per cent of your empty car.
- Tell your insurance company that you will be towing a caravan. Not telling them can affect your cover. Overloading a caravan can also affect your cover.

● Ferry Tales

If you're taking your car to the Continent, the shortest ferry crossing is usually the cheapest – but it's not necessarily the most economical. A longer crossing can mean fewer miles to drive, either in Britain or on the other side, which means less petrol and less stress. If you live in Wales or the West of England, say, it would be silly to drive to Dover if your eventual destination is southern France.

You need to be a maths genius to work out exact costings – ferry prices differ according to the time of year, time of crossing and the car you are driving – and you may prefer to spend more time on the road and less on the water anyway. But you should definitely weigh up all the alternative routes before you book a ferry.

Night crossings: If the ferry crossing you choose takes more than just a few hours, you should consider sailing at night – especially if you have a long drive before you get to the port. Booking a cabin will cost you extra, but you will get a night's sleep, you'll save on one night's accommodation and you'll arrive alert and ready for a full day's driving.

Check-in time: Ferry sailings, just like planes, have a minimum check-in time for motorists. You should aim to arrive before that. In the busy season when the check-in time arrives, the companies start to load the cars on 'stand-by' tickets. If you arrive late, even if you have a confirmed booking, they can refuse to let you board and you'll have to join the stand-by queue for the next crossing (and pray that some families booked on it fail to turn up in time).

Getting a seat: On a busy day on all but the shortest crossings, if you haven't booked a cabin, you should nominate a 'runner' for the family. As soon as you've parked the car on board, the 'runner' should streak off to find seats for you all and reserve them with bags and coats. The slower ones – usually Mum and the toddlers – follow in their own time.

If you plan to eat, shop for duty-frees and change some money during the crossing, eat first. Most people shop first. There are always queues waiting for the duty-free and the *bureau de change* to open, but rarely queues towards the end of the sailing. If you grab a table in a self-service café or a restaurant, you will have seats and a base for as long as you want to linger over your food – and you can send a 'runner' to check on the length of the shopping queues.

Hand luggage: You're not usually allowed back to your car once you've left it on the car deck. So lock it and take with you *everything* you'll need for the crossing. Memorise the number of the deck where your car is and the exit number you use.

• Coach Journeys

As on aircraft, you should travel with all your necessary paperwork and your personal 'life-support system' – anything you'll need during the journey – in your hand luggage. You won't have access to your main case during the journey.

Luggage is usually stored underneath the main body of the coach through side doors. The last case loaded will be the first case out.

Sun and shade: For journeys in hot countries, work out the direction you'll be travelling – north, south, east or west. Then you'll know which side of the coach will be in the direct sunlight. It won't necessarily be the side that's in the sun in the car-park.

The power of the sun is intensified by the window glass. For a cooler, less sticky journey choose the shady side – especially if you're at all prone to travel sickness.

Coach transfers: Most air package holidays involve coach journeys from the foreign airport to your holiday accommodation. If it's a long journey (the holiday company or its brochure should tell you) don't expect a coach with a loo or refreshment or air-conditioning. And don't assume you will be able to buy suitable snacks and drinks at every foreign airport. So allow for the coach leg of your journey when you're packing refreshments.

• Travel Sickness

Stop please, driver. I'm going to be . . . eurrrrgh

There's no poetry in motion sickness. It's horrible. Some people – always those who don't suffer from it – say it's all in the mind. It isn't.

However, it is true that seeing other people throwing up can bring on your own nausea. So can talking about it. Don't talk to children about the possibility of them being sick. (Just take precautions and be ready in case they do go pale and quiet and start feeling sick.)

Many methods of avoiding travel sickness that work for some people are dismissed as 'old wives' tales' by others – yet they do work. It doesn't matter if there's no medical explanation. If one method works for you, stick to it.

- Eat a light non-fatty meal before the journey.
- Avoid fizzy drinks.
- Eat little and often is popular advice – although once the tell-tale symptoms of yawning, the cold sweats and dizziness start, you probably won't be able to swallow much.
- Ginger is a favourite remedy. Try crystallised or stem ginger, or drink a teaspoon of powdered ginger in a glass of fruit juice.
- Another belief is that pressing a point on your wrist prevents motion sickness. You can buy bands that claim to do this.
- Other remedies include chewing gum, chewing glucose tablets and covering your stomach with brown

paper. (Both an Italian and a Yorkshireman tell me they swear by this remedy.)

- I've also read more than once about the effectiveness of pork fat against seasickness. I don't know whether you're supposed to eat it or rub it on your belly.

Wherever possible stay in the fresh air. In cars, open the window. On planes, point the ceiling air nozzles at you. (If you can't get them to work, call the stewardess.) On boats, stay on deck. In coaches, open the windows and, where you can't, organise the overhead air streams to point at you.

Being occupied helps. I sometimes suffer from car and coach sickness but never when I am driving. In cars and coaches, don't play games that involve reading. Better to play something that involves looking through the window.

On boats, keep your eyes on the horizon. If you start to feel ill, lie down if possible and try not to move your head much. If you can't keep your eyes on the horizon, close your eyes and imagine a straight unmoving horizon. Sleep is a good preventive.

When I was compiling notes for this chapter I had to cross to Dublin from Holyhead. It was January and my ferry was cancelled because of the severe gales. Eventually a boat decided to sail. Passengers weren't allowed on deck – it was too rough. I decided to head for the bar but only because I knew there were sofas there. (As it turned out it was too rough to walk across the room to buy a drink.)

I lay down and plugged in my personal stereo. I closed my eyes and concentrated on a straight, still horizon. I'd just read about the wrist pressure-point bands so I held one hand tightly round one wrist. I don't suppose I looked any odder than the other people lying around the place. When we finally docked I still had an unused paper bag! As I limped off the gangplank, the man in front of me knelt down and kissed the ground.

• Holidays with Kids

Are we nearly there, Mum?

When I was putting together a television feature about travelling with children, I asked twenty well-travelled mothers for advice. Fifteen simply said: 'Don't.'

Moving around with children is never easy. All right. It can be hell. What's more, you can spend all that money and effort on going away on holiday and all they talk about once they get home is the funny ice-cream and the day Mummy was sick over the balcony.

But sharing your child's first paddle in the sea, their first ride on a ferry or a plane, is something not to be missed. And as the mother of six-month-old twins said outside her holiday tent in the South of France, 'I have to feed and change them every few hours anyway. It's just so much nicer doing it by a hot beach with a glass of cheap plonk in my hand.'

Some sorts of holidays, and some holiday destinations, are far more suitable for young families than others. Catholic countries give children the warmest welcome. In Spain, France and Italy, push-chairs are commonly seen in all but the grandest restaurants. In Ireland children can join you in most pubs.

'Blind date' holidays are definitely *not* so suitable if you have kids in tow. These are the cheap offers, usually booked at the last minute, which don't name your accommodation until you arrive. Fine for the freewheeling independent traveller. Not so fine if you're taking a push-chair and a toddler and you find you're up at the top of a steep hill the wrong side of the motorway from the beach.

Be prepared for children to get disorientated on holiday and forget what they have recently learned. Toddlers who've been toilet trained can need nappies again while they are away. A child who is well drilled in road safety can suddenly wander out into the road.

On foreign package holidays there's usually a set charge of £15 or so for babies under two. You then pay the hotel direct for hiring a cot and for any baby food. In family hotels cot charges are around £1 a night. Smarter hotels that don't encourage family bookings will charge you £10 a night.

It is possible to buy some familiar baby-food brands in some countries abroad – but don't rely on this unless you or a reliable friend have been to the resort before. Take your own supplies especially if your little one is a fussy eater.

Use a lie-back buggy if possible. (Borrow one or swap your sit-up one for the holiday if you don't own your own.) Lie-back buggies are better for sleeping in restaurants, trains and departure lounges. If you're planning on taking a travel cot, use it for a week or two at home before you go away, so that baby will be used to it. (It'll probably be safer than using a foreign cot. See page 125 on safety.)

The journey: It may be fine when you get there – but it's often the travelling from home to your holiday destination that puts years on parents. Military-style planning and preparation is essential.

- Don't forget to put your children on your passport and insure them. See p. 77.
- Leave home prepared for the worst. Travel equipped to handle monsoons, heatwaves, a big freeze and a ten-hour delay. The worst that will then happen will be a broken fingernail.
- Time your journey accurately before preparing for it. OK, so it's only a two-hour flight from your London airport to Spain – but add on getting to and from the airports, your check-in time, the wait for your luggage and your transfer coach and you could well be

on the road for ten hours or longer, and that's without any unscheduled delays. Prepare accordingly.

- Always ask for help. People hardly ever volunteer to help a parent who's loaded down with luggage and children. But pluck up courage to ask for help and passers-by rarely refuse.

- Label your child with their name and destination and, if applicable, flight number. In the thirty seconds it takes you to search your bag for your tickets, a small child will have nipped round a corner and out of sight. Many travelling parents insist on leading reins for toddlers.

- Label their favourite toy, too. Grown-ups have been known to have to make hundred-mile detours when precious teddy has been left in a motorway cafe. What if there was no time to back-track *and* catch the ferry you've booked?

- Load your bag with tiny, inexpensive treats. Produce them at intervals just as they're about to reach their boredom threshold. Wrap up each treat – if you can find the time – because gift-wrapping makes the treats more exciting. Avoid chocolate if you're heading for somewhere hot.

- Take games to play on the journey, but not games with pieces that can get lost. They will.

- In your hand luggage pack a change of clothes for each child along with their favourite toy or toys. Planes especially can be either hot or chilly. You'll need at least one layer of clothes to peel off or put on.

- Breast-fed babies are the easiest children to cater for on journeys and on holiday. If your baby is due to be weaned, wait till after the holiday.

- If baby is bottle-fed, label the bottles you make up for the journey with his/her name and its contents. If the cabin crew are warming up more than one bottle, there will be no chance of a mix-up.

- Test-drive a training mug before you set out. Many are not leak-proof. Put clingfilm under the lid to make it leak-proof, so you can travel with a drink at the ready.

- Sleep is more important for children than food. Don't wake them up for a meal unless you know you're not going to be near food and drink again for hours. Carry their favourite snacks and drinks with you. (You can go back to a more balanced sensible diet after the holiday.)

Flying: Night-time flights can be a false economy when you're travelling with children. For the journey home, you may well have to leave your accommodation by midday. The money you spend on snacks, drinks and keeping everyone entertained between leaving your room and boarding the plane will be as much as the supplement for a daytime flight. Sadly, however, if you do pay extra for a daytime flight and the flight is delayed into the night, the company won't repay your supplement.

Children under two travel for a nominal fee but aren't entitled to their own seat or their own baggage allowance – although you are allowed to take a baby bag on board, with their necessities for the journey. If the plane is full, they must travel on your knee.

Older children who are on a 'free' holiday do get their own seat and a full baggage allowance.

Check in early so you can all sit together and make sure the check-in staff know you're travelling with children. If the plane is not full, ask to be next to an empty seat.

Ask at the airport whether there are any special mother and baby facilities. Standards and facilities vary enormously in British airports and around the world. Some mother and baby rooms have kettles, bottle-warmers, toys and nappy-changing tables. Many don't. Some are so poorly advertised and signposted that they never get used. (More than once I've escaped babyless from an overcrowded ladies' loo to an empty mothers' room to put on my make-up in peace.) If there are no mother and baby facilities, look for a loo for the disabled. They are roomier than normal ones and have enough space for a pushchair.

Book a baby cot for long journeys. Order it in advance. These cots are not big – around twenty-five inches long – and they're usually fixed at the bulkhead. So you'll be sitting in the front row of a section – which means if you try to watch the film you'll have a poor view and a stiff neck.

If you're taking your own carry-cot, phone the airline in advance to tell them its measurements and ask whether it will be allowed on board. Babies aren't allowed to stay in their cots during take-offs and landings. You must hold them in your arms.

If you'll be breast-feeding during the journey, tell the check-in people. They might find a suitable quiet seat for you. Some cabin crews let mothers breast-feed in the privacy of the crew's curtained-off section. Some don't. Take a shawl to wrap round you for a little privacy if you want it. Have a small plastic bottle of water or a carton of juice with a straw for yourself to drink as the crew can be very slow at getting round to delivering the in-flight drinks.

For bottle-feeding, take a made-up, labelled bottle on board and ask the crew to warm it up. Have an extra bottle made-up in case of unscheduled delays.

Feed baby before cabin meal-times. The crew then should have time to help you if need be.

A few scheduled airlines offer special children's meals. You need to book these in advance through your travel agent or directly with the airline. It's best to double-check any special orders for meals with the airline two days before the flight.

Some scheduled airlines carry supplies of disposable nappies. Some don't. Carry your own supply of nappies with you and a roll of plastic bags for used ones.

Some airlines claim that it's possible to change a baby's nappy in the loo. These loos were obviously not designed by a woman. If there's no queue for the loo, you can try changing baby on the floor outside the toilets. Use your duty-free plastic carrier to lay them on. Otherwise travel with a changing bag that unzips to become a changing mat.

Keep hold of your push-chair as long as possible. It's nearly always a marathon walk from the check-in desk to the plane. Most airlines let you keep a push-chair with you until you board. The crew then stow it away and hand it back as you disembark. (Don't depend on it for hanging extra bags on that you won't be able to carry up any plane stairs.)

Ask the crew if your children can visit the flight-deck during the flight. Pilots on holiday charter flights are especially good at allowing children this treat – but don't expect to be allowed up front when the crew are serving meals or selling the duty-frees.

Children suffer less than adults from jet-lag. (For one thing, it's easier for them to sleep in a plane seat.) They do however suffer more from dehydration than adults. See they have plenty to drink during the flight.

Children can suffer from painful ear-ache during take off and landing. Give them something to suck. For a baby, the best relief is crying! Children with colds are especially vulnerable.

A Qantas Airways publicity hand-out says: 'It's handy to recognise that babies and small children will not adjust their behaviour for the convenience of others. Accept this, most other passengers will.'

On the road: There are two ways to tackle a long car journey. The first is to tuck them in the back with blankets and pillows, kiss them goodnight and drive with your foot down through the night to your destination. The children should arrive almost fresh, alert and happy. The driver and navigator, however, could be walking zombies for a day or two.

The other method is to make the journey as much fun as possible and a big part of the holiday. You drive through the day – more traffic but less of a break from normal waking/sleeping routine – and make frequent short stops for walks, picnics and visits to places of interest. During the journey all but tiny babies and the driver will have to be entertained.

- Load the car with cassettes and story tapes. Your local library may stock some you can borrow.
- Invent games that involve looking out of the car window. (The first one to spot six red cars . . .)
- Avoid reading in the car. It makes for car sickness. See page 101.
- Have a sheet, a towel or a shawl to hand. Fix it over a back side window to screen children and babies from hot, strong sunlight.
- If you're hiring a car abroad, order a car safety seat or child restraint. You will have to book it well in advance, especially for holidays in July and August. Don't expect small local car hire companies to have them.
- Only travel with a carry-cot on the back seat if you can fix it with a proper harness.

Coaches: Most coach holiday companies won't take small children on their tours. But most air package holidays use coaches to transfer you from the airport to your holiday accommodation. A child who isn't prone to car sickness can be affected by coach travel. Don't mention the possibility to your children (plant the idea in their heads and they're halfway to throwing up) but stop them from reading on the coach.

Ferries: On the way to the port, when you're planning your loo and snack stops, allow for a long wait on the quayside before you get to drive on to the ferry or hovercraft. A Rice Rule decrees, of course, that the further away from the toilet you are, the more a child will want one.

Some ferries have entertainment for children on board – kids' cartoon films in a cinema and junior discos. Some have mother and baby rooms.

On ferries you and your children are free to roam around. Hovercrafts, though, are much more like planes. Everyone is assigned a seat, which are in rows, and you are encouraged to stay in it.

If at all possible, use the loos only at the beginning of a ferry journey. Unless the sea is mill-pond flat, the loos get more and more unpleasant with every turbulent wave. On rough crossings, if you're not ill as you enter the toilets, you will be as you leave. Young children's stomachs, however, are rarely affected by all this.

As a rule, you're not allowed to go back to your car during the crossing. Take everything you may need from the car. Don't expect the ferry shops to sell nappies or baby food.

On longer day crossings, consider booking a day cabin. With your own cabin you won't have to rush to 'bag' seats when you first get on board and then have to guard them and your hand luggage for the whole journey. You can also breast-feed and change baby in peace and privacy. Book your day cabin in advance, and when you book let the company know you're travelling with a small child or children and tell them you want to avoid as many steep stairs between decks as possible.

Trains: Avoid travelling on summer Saturdays. Crowded holiday trains are hell on earth and no way to start a holiday.

Always make seat reservations in advance. Children under five travel free on British Rail – but you can't reserve a seat for them.

Consider buying a family railcard (£20 in 1990) which entitles up to four adults to travel at a third or a half discount and up to four children, aged fourteen and under, to travel at £1 each. With a £1 ticket a child can then have a seat reservation. People travelling together on a family railcard don't have to be related. Book seat reservations for weekend summer travel well in advance.

Special Holiday Maker trains – usually to and from Scotland, North Wales and the West of England – have seat reservations for every seat. Without a reservation you have to stand – unless there are any no-shows. You can take children under five for free on Holiday Makers, but they won't have a guaranteed seat. These trains can get booked up some weeks in advance.

Seat reservations on Holiday Makers are free. On other trains they currently cost £1 a seat, standard class, but you can reserve up to four seats together for a total of £1.

Buy your tickets for Holiday Maker trains before May if you can. British Rail Saver fares usually go up in May and down again in October. If you travel in the summer months but you've bought your ticket before the fares went up, you don't pay the higher price.

Never assume that a buffet will be open.

Don't expect clean, hygienic toilets in stations or on trains. For changing nappies and breast-feeding babies, your best bet is a station with a Women Only waiting room. At least the other passengers will be sympathetic.

Some of the new InterCity trains have fold-down tables in the loo where you could just about change a baby's nappy. Other train loos are impossible. Whenever you can, change baby at the station.

In France in the summer there are occasional 'family' trains which are equipped to entertain children. They have a play area and a nursery area.

A rucksack leaves your hands free for children and push-chairs. A baby in a sling or backpack leaves your hands free for bags and opening train doors. If your journey doesn't start at a terminus, you won't have long to load yourself, possessions and family on to the train.

Pregnant travellers: Check that your travel insurance policy covers you if you're pregnant, and if it does, up to how many weeks pregnant.

If you're flying, check the policy of the airline. Some won't fly women who are more than twenty-eight weeks pregnant. Others will fly women who will be up to thirty-two weeks pregnant on the return journey. After twenty-eight weeks, you may well have to get a medical certificate.

Don't take any travel sickness pills without first checking with your doctor.

• Boats

Taking to the waters

You don't have to own your own boat to spend your holidays afloat. You don't even have to have any sailing experience. Complete novices can hire a canal narrow-boat or a river cruiser at home or abroad.

You don't even need any sailing experience to be able to holiday on a small yacht if you buy a 'villa flotilla' holiday. You spend the first week learning to sail and sleeping on land, and the second, sailing the seas with a group of other boats. You meet up in the evenings and there's an experienced leader in the group to offer help if you need it. If you or someone you are holidaying with can sail a dinghy, you can join a flotilla straight away.

Bareboating: You have to be an experienced sailor to hire a sailing boat and sail off independently on to the high seas. Don't lie about your experience. If you need to have the expression 'bareboat charter' explained, then you aren't yet enough of a sailor to be allowed to holiday this way.

Companies usually ask for a 'declaration of experience' when you book a bareboat charter and they have the right not to let you sail if you turn up having lied about your sailing prowess. The boat people say they can tell as soon as someone steps aboard whether or not they know what they are doing. A false 'declaration of experience' can also invalidate your insurance.

Luggage for landlubbers: If you've never been boating before, you might not realise just how little storage space there is on board. Unless you're staying in a suite on a millionaire's floating gin palace, don't take a proper suitcase. Take a light soft-sided case that you can squash into any shaped cupboard.

In Britain, boaties pack everything in carrier bags and plastic dustbin liners, although if you're driving to the boatyard you could always unpack your suitcase there before you cast off and leave your empty case in the car boot.

What to take: Pack as little as possible. There won't be room to store many outfits. In hot weather you'll be able to dry your washed clothes in an hour or so. In cold weather you can keep warm by wearing all the clothes you've brought in layers.

Experienced boaters are always the scruffiest people on the water. They are also the warmest and the driest. Pack a lightweight windproof, waterproof jacket and a sweater. For everywhere except the tropics (and especially on European rivers) you must be ready for chilly early mornings and late evenings.

Shoes: On board any small boat you need flat, non-slip rubber-soled or rope-soled shoes. Any other sort might cause you to slip on a wet deck and – equally important – might damage the boat.

If you're dressing up for a trip on shore, don't put smooth-soled or high-heeled shoes on until you're off the boat.

Entertainment: Take your own entertainment. Unless you are certain that you can moor up each night somewhere where there's a restaurant, a bar or some night-life, you'll be glad of a cassette player or radio, a pack of cards or Trivial Pursuit.

Everything shipshape: Tidy boaters are happy boaters. In the confined space of a boat you need to be tidy to be comfortable. Uncleaned, slippery decks and stuff left lying around on them can cause accidents.

Don't be embarrassed to set up some sort of routine from the start. You don't have to ram your boat rules down everyone's throat but if you all put things away when you've used them, I promise you, life on board will be more bearable.

Health and safety afloat: On Day One, work out between you exactly what your drill will be if someone falls overboard.

Cot-bound babies are safe enough on board. Obedient and keen older children are fine, too. It's toddlers and small children you should worry about. You will need to see that they *always* wear a buoyancy aid when they're on deck and that they're never left alone up on deck.

Remember that the sun's rays are stronger when they're reflected off water. A cooling sea breeze disguises just how hot the sun is. Protect your skin as described on pages 129–133.

If you invite extra people on board and you stay below deck, be certain that you have adequate ventilation. Canal and river boats especially have virtually draughtproof windows. Keep them open when you entertain guests.

Never sleep in a cabin with a gas heater burning.

Booking a boat: If you can afford it, book a boat with more berths (beds) than you need. Small boats are never roomy and two people in a three- or four-berth boat will be glad of the extra space.

Before you book consider this: life on board is 'intimate' and one of the fastest and most accurate ways of testing a relationship. If your marriage or affair is going through a rough patch, a holiday cooped together on a small boat will be make-or-break time.

How far to go: You invariably have to return your craft to wherever you first boarded it. Be conservative when you're planning how far to travel. Take the advice of the people at the boatyard. Allow more time for getting back than you needed for the outward journey. Many a holiday has been spoilt on the last day or so by worrying about making it back in time.

• Health

Whose idea was it to have the prawns?

As package holiday destinations become more exotic, so do the illnesses you can succumb to. When I first started travelling I would wander off abroad with a cavalier belief that all this travel was building up my body's natural resistance to all foreign bugs. Then I sailed down the Nile. I flew home loaded with some wonderful baubles, some glorious photographs and a bug that laid me out for 12 months.

As it happens, I couldn't have been inoculated against this particular delight but if I'd been more careful about what I'd eaten and drunk, and where and from what, I would have been saved a year of feeling like a washed-out rag. I couldn't even drown my sorrows because alcohol was taboo while I was taking the tablets.

When I first got back from the trip I thought that the sickness and the runs would clear up of their own accord. The doctors at London's Tropical Diseases Hospital told me that if I'd waited much longer before coming for treatment I might never have been fully cured. My mind and bowels still boggle at the thought. Aren't holidays fun?

Please don't let my experience scare you, and don't let this long list of do's and don'ts put you off leaving Britain. Just remember that it's better to be safe than sick and sore.

Jabs: Don't trust the holiday companies, the tourist offices or the travel agents to tell you what inoculations you might need. Some only tell you what is compulsory (which is very little) and don't let you know about what the health authorities very strongly recommend. Some simply don't know. And some think that just mentioning jabs will put you off booking the holiday.

Don't expect your GP or local chemist to know all the requirements for all the countries in the world, either. There are vaccination centres run by people like Thomas Cook and British Airways which offer up-to-date advice on what's compulsory and what's recommended. They should tell you over the phone for free. The Department of Health publishes a free leaflet of information.

So find out exactly what inoculations are recommended for the place you're going to and start organising your jabs two months before you leave. Some involve a course of injections spread over weeks.

Mosquitoes and other pesky critters: If you're planning to go to a country where there might be malaria, at least three weeks before you leave get professional advice on *which* anti-malaria tablets to take. The good specialist travel companies advise their clients, or you should ask a vaccination centre. You can buy the tablets you'll need from a chemist without a prescription.

There is more than one kind of anti-malaria treatment to take and it's essential you choose the right one for the country you're visiting. I once asked a pharmacist which tablets I needed for a particular country. A day or two later I discovered he'd sold me the wrong ones. I went back to tell him, to get the right ones I needed and to stop him giving the wrong advice to other customers. He apologised – and admitted that he'd once given his mother the wrong pills and she came back from her holiday with malaria.

You need to start taking malaria tablets about two weeks before the trip and continue taking them for some weeks after you get home. Do this even if you don't think you were bitten. Some tablets you take weekly, others daily. Take the daily tablets at the same time every day (allowing for the jump forward or back in time during the journey). For weekly tablets, write yourself a reminder note and keep it near your toothbrush, razor or something you use every day.

Even when you're taking the tablets you should avoid being bitten by mosquitoes. You'll want to anyway, because the bites can itch like hell.

- Mosquitoes are most active towards evening and after dark. Be ready for them by dusk.
- Travel with the sort of mosquito repellent that plugs into a two-pin electric socket. You feed it a fresh tablet at dusk and leave it plugged in all night.
- As an alternative, in many malarial countries you can buy anti-mosquito coils which you light up at dusk and let burn through the night. They don't smell so wonderful but they keep the beasts at bay.
- Leave off wearing perfumes, aftershaves and perfumed deodorants. They attract mossies and midges.
- Don't leave a light on in your room if you go out at night. It attracts flying pests.
- From dusk onwards, cover *all* exposed flesh with insect repellent (which smells and tastes disgusting).
- You should cover up as much of your body as possible in the evening. This isn't what you want on holiday, I know, but in malaria areas it really does make sense for women to pack trousers and long-sleeved tops for evening wear. In non-malaria areas you'll probably still be glad of the cover-ups. You can always save the backless number for showing off your tan back home.
- You can buy sporty-looking wrist and ankle bands soaked in an insect repellent called diethyl toluamide. Look for the name on the products you buy. Chemists are very reluctant to sell the chemical separately so you're better off buying ready-prepared 'buzz bands' than trying to make your own.
- Less effective but sweeter-smelling as an insect repellant is citronella oil.

Malaria symptoms are similar to flu and can develop a good time after you're bitten. So if you feel feverish and fluish some weeks after your intrepid trip, don't forget to tell your doctor where you've been.

First-aid kit: See page 44 about what to pack as a matter of course to cover minor ailments and deal with cuts and bruises.

These days, there's a growing awareness that it's not always a good idea to have an injection abroad. For one thing, a needle that's been used before can transfer Aids. If the idea scares you – and it should – you can take your own surgical supplies with you, thanks to the Medical Advisory Service for Travellers Abroad. The MASTA kit, popularly called the 'Aids Pack', contains sterilised needles, sutures, syringes and swabs – very reassuring if you have to have an injection or stitches abroad. It currently costs £12 from British Airways travel clinics and from MASTA, London School of Hygiene and Tropical Medicine, Keppel Street, London WC1E 7HT. (Telephone 071–631 4408 for full details.)

A dose of your own medicine: Some countries forbid the import of substances that can be found in a few medicines prescribed in Britain. If you need to take prescribed, strong medicaments – especially ones containing morphine – it's sensible to keep the treatment in its original container showing the chemist's label.

Travel with no more than you will need for your stay away. A letter from your doctor explaining why you must take your medicine is also a sensible precaution. Keep this medicine secure at all times, especially any treatment that at home you would lock away from children.

Water: In many places in the world – including many parts of Europe – the tap water can be hostile to the British constitution. Its harmful effects can be anything from a slightly upset stomach to a serious illness. Take advice from your holiday rep, if you have one, or seek information from other visitors (the natives might be immune). It's more important to heed one person who's been made ill by the water than a dozen who say, 'It's never done me any harm'. If you're at all unsure about what comes out of the tap:

- Drink bottled mineral water – but not from a bottle that has already been opened.
- Don't take ice in your drinks – freezing the water doesn't kill all the bugs.
- Don't eat locally-made ices and ice-lollies.
- Peel fruit before you eat it.
- Or wash fruit and vegetables in water that you know is clean.
- Don't drink from cracked or dirty cups and glasses.
- Keep your mouth shut when you're swimming – in pools as well as the sea.

To purify water: You can sterilise water by fast-boiling it for ten minutes. If you have no means of boiling it, you can buy sterilising tablets from a chemist's. Keep them in a tightly-capped bottle or they will quickly lose their purifying power.

Alternatively, you can use iodine to sterilise water. You buy it from a chemist as crystals, tablets or a two per cent tincture that comes in a dropper. Follow the chemist's instructions and use a plastic screw-top bottle for mixing the water and iodine. Shake the bottle for a thorough mix. You need to let it stand for 15–20 minutes before drinking – longer if the water is very cold. Before you go away, try drinking water you have sterilised to check that you're not allergic to iodine.

Though it's often suggested as an attractive alternative, I'm sorry to have to tell you that alcohol does not sterilise water.

Eating out: Just because a hotel or restaurant is expensive, that doesn't mean that its kitchens are clean and safe. I've secretly nosed around the kitchens and backyards of too many posh places ever to believe that it could.

- You are most at risk from food that has been cooked, stored and then reheated.
- Food in restaurants and cafés with a fast turnover is safest.
- Choose stews for lunch when they are newly made,

not for supper when they may have been standing around all day.

- Freshly cooked foods are the safest to eat. Shellfish and undercooked meat cause the most problems.
- Don't eat badly bruised or damaged fruit and vegetables.
- Don't drink unpasteurised milk unless it has been boiled.

Diarrhoea: Many medics say that ordinary 'tourist's' diarrhoea is best left untreated and will usually right itself in two or three days. But you may not want to spend two or three days of your holiday cringing near the loo, so take the recommended dose of the anti-diarrhoea treatment you brought with you from a British chemist's.

- Eat bland foods like dry bread and rice until it's fully cleared up. You probably won't be able to face anything else.
- Keep drinking plenty of fluids – but not alcohol. Still drinks are better than fizzy ones.
- The contraceptive pill can lose its effect with vomiting or diarrhoea. Take other precautions.
- If a baby under a year old gets an attack of diarrhoea, get medical help and, until help arrives, try to get them to drink some fluid.

Camomile tea is noted for soothing slightly upset stomachs. Travel with some camomile tea-bags. Constipation is less common when you're abroad. Alleviate it with plenty of fruit and leafy vegetables.

Bites and stings: Read the advice I've already given on mosquitoes and malaria – the same repellants can keep other insects at bay. But if you do get bitten . . .

- Use an ice-cube to soothe a bite or sting.
- If a sting is visible in the flesh, get it out using tweezers or clean fingernails. Then scrub the area clean.
- Use sodium bicarbonate on bee stings, vinegar or

lemon juice on wasp and hornet stings. Remember B for Bicarb and Bees, V for Vinegar, Very sour lemons and Vasps. Don't mix the remedies, they don't work.

- If you're stung by a jellyfish, rub wet sand over your skin to remove any tentacles stuck to you. You can soothe a jellyfish sting with diluted ammonia. You find diluted ammonia in urine. I suppose it depends on how desperate you are. Lemon juice can relieve the bite instead. In the tropics, use the skin of the paw-paw fruit.

- If you're sharing the sea with sea urchins, always wear plastic shoes. If you step on a sea urchin with bare feet you'll know about it at once. Use baby lotion, olive oil or whatever cream or oil you have to hand to help the spine work its way out of your flesh. Then go and buy a pair of plastic shoes.

You may realise with horror one night that you're sharing your room with many unwanted tiny strangers – bedbugs. They will have been living in cracks in the wall, under the wallpaper, in the bed frame or under the carpet. Move the bed away from the wall. Keep the light on – these creatures prefer to feast in the dark.

Other unpleasant animals: Avoid making friends with animals abroad. The risk of rabies is very real. If you get scratched or bitten by an animal, or one licks an open cut or graze, hold the wound under running water and scrub with soap or detergent for a good five minutes. Rinse and soak it in gin or whisky. Get medical help as soon as possible.

That's one reason why you should never pose for photographs with monkeys, parrots or other exotic animals at resorts. You can catch all sorts of things from them. The other reason is that you shouldn't encourage this cruel enterprise. The animals are usually kept in appalling conditions and have a short life expectancy.

Snakes only strike at moving objects. If you see one, keep absolutely still.

Aids: Don't believe anybody who says that there is no Aids in their country. How do they know? Has everybody living there and every visitor been tested in the last week?

When you're organising your holiday inoculations consider having jabs against tetanus. Then if you suffer a dubious gash you won't need a local anti-tetanus jab. These days, in all but the most organised, sophisticated countries, it's wise to avoid needles of any sort.

When I go along to the immunisation centre these days, the worldly-wise doctor now ends his 'Have a good trip' speech with a warning not to have my ears pierced or get tattooed when I'm away. I won't and neither should you. You don't know where the needles have been.

If there's the slightest, weeniest, remotest chance that, against all official and unofficial advice, you will have yourself a holiday romance with someone other than a regular long-term partner, travel with some condoms in your wallet or purse. Don't rely on being able to buy them near your holiday bed. Lecture over.

Miscellaneous maladies

- For a sore throat, gargle with a glass of warm water mixed with a teaspoon of salt.
- If there's no clean water available for washing a wound, use cold tea, beer or a soft drink.
- Use neat alcohol – vodka, gin, whisky – as an emergency medical disinfectant on cuts and grazes.
- In emergencies, toothpaste can be used as an antiseptic cream.
- For a sudden toothache, use a plug of cotton-wool soaked in oil of cloves. If you haven't brought any oil of cloves in your first-aid kit, look for cloves in the market or in a restaurant kitchen. Wedge the clove near the source of the pain (usually a missing filling) and chew on it for some relief.
- For sore inflamed gums, swill the mouth with a teaspoon of salt in a glass of warm drinking water.
- In hot, humid weather women can develop thrush, which is uncomfortable and unpleasant. Avoid syn-

thetic underwear. Stick to cotton and apply yoghurt as a soother and a healer.

- A lot of sexual activity on holiday can cause a sudden attack of cystitis in women, which gives a burning sensation when you pee. (It used to be called the 'honeymoon disease'.) You need to drink plenty of fluids – and cranberry juice, if you can get it, is supposed to be particularly effective. Failing that, any citrus fruit juice can help alter the acidity of your urine and stop the burning sensation

Lethal bush: Oleander, the bush with pretty pink flowers, sometimes called the rose-bay bush, grows wild around the Mediterranean. And it's seriously poisonous. Don't let children play near it – they can develop a bad rash and, if they eat the flowers, can die. Don't ever put its branches on a bonfire. The fumes from the smoke are poisonous. And don't ever use the branches as barbecue meat skewers. It has been known to happen and, I'm told, the picnickers died.

Deep trouble: If your holiday includes scuba-diving, you should not fly within twenty-four hours of diving to any depth greater than thirty feet. If you do, you're liable to suffer the serious consequences of decompression sickness – the bends. No reputable scuba diving school or club will let you dive deep the day before you fly home.

Security: Never leave medicines, insect repellents and strong substances like bleach and ant powder lying around where children could get to them. Lock them away and be as vigilant as you would be at home.

Back home: If you develop a fever or flu-like symptoms after your holiday, or you just feel unwell, don't take any chances. See your doctor and tell him/her where you've been.

• Playing Safe

Reading this chapter could make you decide to stay at home and decorate the kitchen. Don't. Holidays aren't really dangerous things. More horrible accidents take place in the home than ever happen on holiday. This chapter just points you towards all the things that *could* happen. Anyway isn't there something about prevention being better than cure?

HOTEL HORRORS

Glass doors: Glass doors abroad don't always comply with British safety standards – they may not be made of laminated or toughened safety glass. If there's a large glass door in your hotel room or apartment, stick large labels on it at eye-level – yours and a child's – so that you can see at a glance that it's closed. Walking through a non-safety-glass door in the mistaken belief that it's open can have horrific and bloody consequences.

Lifts: Three-sided lifts are dangerous. Never let children use one without an adult with them. Keep clear of the missing side when you are in one. People (and children especially) have lost limbs by catching their clothes between the moving lift and the lift shaft.

Floors: Watch out for slippery floors – a common feature in hot-climate hotels. Marble, polished tiles or stone can be dangerously slippery especially when wet. Don't run on one.

Balconies: Check whether your children could squeeze

through the bars. Check how secure the railings are. Falling off dodgy balconies is a common holiday death.

Cots: Don't use a cot that has a gap between the side and the mattress where your baby's head could get stuck. Check the width of the side bars. Are they too wide? Could your child's head get stuck? Are there any sharp bits? Babies have been strangled by their clothing getting caught up in cots. If the hotel won't – or can't – change the cot for a safe one, plug the gap between mattress and sides with rolled up towels or clothes. Securely wrap the sides with towels or blankets – easier said than done. As an alternative to a dangerous cot, small babies can sleep in a drawer, either on a table or on the floor.

Electricity: Cover dodgy sockets with sticky tape and then heavy furniture to stop children getting at them.

Gas: Has the gas appliance in your apartment got an up-to-date safety certificate? Even if it has, always make sure there is adequate ventilation in every room. Never close all the windows and doors when the gas is on.

Fire: Memorise the route from your bedroom to the nearest fire exit. I have heard of one fire officer (a man paid to know about these things) who won't sleep in a strange room on holiday until he has memorised the escape route by *crawling* to the fire exit with his eyes closed.

- During a fire, the clearest air is nearest to the floor.
- The wetter a room is, the slower it burns. Put plugs in the bath and washbasin and run all the taps.
- Leave your room with a wet towel round your mouth and nose.
- Keep the key in the door when you are in a locked room.
- Report any blocked or locked fire escapes and get them seen to. Nag the hotel manager and make a nuisance of yourself until they are clear.

Also be wary of . . .

- Staircases without handrails or with large gaps in the banisters
- Frayed electrical wires
- Light-switches in a bathroom
- Swimming pools with no depth markers
- Swimming pools without a slip-resistant surround.

PROTECT YOUR INTERESTS

Theft in hotels: If your hotel doesn't offer a reliable safety box, when you leave your room hang out the 'Do not disturb' notice and don't leave your key in reception. The 'Make up my room' notice and a key hanging by its room number in reception are useful advertisements to a thief. Lock your valuables in a hard-sided case and possibly pad-lock the case to heavy furniture.

Divide your wealth: Never carry all your valuables in one pocket. Divide them around pockets. Better still, divide them around your party when you're not travelling alone. Never keep a wallet or cash in a trouser back pocket. The side slit pockets are safer. If you're going anywhere where there are likely to be pickpockets, secure your pocket with a Velcro fastener. You can *hear* a thief opening the pocket.

Mugging money: Copy the New Yorkers who carry their credit cards in their shoe and a little 'mugging' cash in a pocket to hand over.

Money belts: Nylon money belts make you sweat. Cotton ones are better. You can make a secret money pocket by doubling up an elasticated tube bandage and wearing it on your leg under trousers. Tuck notes and credit cards in the fold.

Shoulder bags: If you're carrying a shoulder bag, pass the strap over your head, so that it rests across your chest. Then tuck the bag under your arm.

Don't advertise: Never count your money in public. At

home, you wouldn't flash a fistful of £10 notes, would you? Don't catch yourself doing the same with foreign money abroad. Learn to recognise the different valued notes as soon as you get them – but in private. Separate the small denomination notes from the high value notes, so that you never accidentally tip someone £50 instead of 50p.

Bags and driving: Keep bags out of sight under the seat to prevent a smash-and-grab when you're stopped in traffic.

Con tricks: Far more people are tricked into giving money to believable con-men (and women, and children) than ever report the matter to the police. Being caught out makes you feel so foolish, many of us just keep quiet.

A very plausible 'student' in Nairobi once asked to join me and a friend for a drink because he wanted 'to practise his English'. We were pleased to talk to a local about his everyday life in Kenya. His long story ended with an involved tale about urgently needing money to help oppressed friends. We were pretty suspicious at the time and sure enough we later found that his story had been tried out for months on other new arrivals. He is probably still working it.

In future I shall take advice I've read from traveller John Hatt. He rightly points out that the crunch always comes when your new-found friend says: 'Don't you trust me?' It's very natural and very British to answer: 'Well, of course' – which gives the con-man the green light to make all types of unreasonable demands. The best answer, says John Hatt, is: 'No, I'm sorry, I don't trust you. I don't trust anyone unless I have continually known them for ten years and I have only known you for five minutes.'

Handing over money for something to be posted on to you is a common way of waving goodbye to your cash. Only do such business with reputable traders.

Insurance: If you're travelling alone, make sure that someone, probably your holiday rep, knows that you have a full insurance policy with a twenty-four-hour emergency number. (You have, haven't you? See page 63.) If they have the number, and you are out for the count, they telephone for funds for hospital treatment and possible repatriation.

Days out: If you plan a long hike off the beaten track, or a day's sailing piloting your own boat, tell someone your plans and the time you think you'll be back. If you don't turn up back at the ranch, they can raise the alarm.

Lilos: Don't doze on a lilo on the sea. Apart from the risk of serious sunburn, you may wake up ten miles from the shore. If you must take to the sea on an inflatable, tell someone on the beach what you're doing and ask them to keep an eye out for you.

Mopeds: The joy and the freedom of the open country road, warm fresh air, hair streaming in the wind, that lovely local wine you had for lunch . . . Holidaymakers and hired mopeds don't mix well. What with the lamentable state of the hired machines, and the roads, and our inexperience at driving the things, not to mention alcohol, perhaps it's not surprising there are so many accidents. The killjoy truth is that in Corfu, to take just one example, the moped is the biggest killer of holidaymakers.

• Beware of the Sun

Most people's priorities for a holiday put warm, sunny weather near the top of the list. And most people going to a sunny climate go with the intention of getting a suntan. That's why most people ignore one of the cardinal rules of holiday health: don't lie around in the sun.

By now you must have heard about how suntanning can cause irreparable damage to your skin and is a cause of skin cancer. If you want to sunbathe because you envy the appearance of those deeply tanned beach belles, well, come back in twenty years and I'll show you some dried-up, wrinkled and leathery bodies. If you think a suntan is sexy, try making love with sunburn. It's painful enough to put the kybosh on any holiday romance.

In Victorian days, only lowly peasants had suntans. A pale skin was a sign of distinction. It showed that you didn't have to toil outside for your keep. It was fashion designer Coco Chanel who, in the 1920s when only the very rich could afford to lounge around in warm foreign climates, decreed that a woman's most essential fashion accessory was a suntan. Ms Chanel didn't know about skin cancer.

Despite all that, I know I'm not going to convince you not to sunbathe. I haven't even convinced myself. But nowadays I do take every precaution I can to protect myself.

I'm a pale redhead and in sunny climes I have to lather myself up with sunscreen almost before I open the curtains in the morning. Even with maximum protection all over my body, I never stay out in the sun for too long. It's a bore but I vow I'll never burn again.

Tanning tips: Make sure you have plenty of suntan oil or cream with you, of the right strength for the amount of sun you'll be getting. Protect yourself strongly at the beginning of the holiday, and let more sun reach you as it goes on.

There's no standard agreement among the cosmetic companies for their sunscreen 'factor' numbers. One company's Factor 4 can be another's Factor 3. The more sensitive your skin, the higher the factor number you need.

- Slap it on all over. Don't forget the odd sensitive areas, like a bald patch on the head, the nape of the neck, the tops of your feet and women's nipples. (The first time I had my hair cut very short I burnt my ears.)

- Blondes don't have more fun. Usually, the paler you are, the more likely you are to burn.

- Take lunch in the shade. The sun's rays are most intense (and so can do the most damage) from 11 a.m. till 3 p.m.

- Beware of the breeze. A cooling breeze stops you feeling the pain and noticing that you are burning.

- Beware of the clouds. In hot climates the sun can burn you even through overcast skies.

- Don't fall asleep in the hot sun. On one beach in Surfer's Paradise in Queensland, Australia, they've rigged up a Tannoy system. Every fifteen minutes a voice booms out: 'Time to turn before you burn.'

- Damp skins burn more easily than dry ones.

- To tell if you're getting too much sun, press your finger on your exposed skin. If it leaves a white mark visible for longer than two seconds you're in danger of burning.

- Save home-made oil and lemon 'suntan' mixes for the salad. These mixes, which you still see young continentals using, contain no sunscreen whatsoever. Neither does the coconut oil you see the locals selling in the tropics.

- It is a myth that you turn a better brown if you first burn red.

It's not only on the beach that the sun can get you. When you're swimming – and especially snorkelling – you're still at risk. The water is cooling, the fish are fascinating and you don't notice that your back is on fire. You should wear at least a T-shirt in the water, and experienced snorkellers often wear old pyjamas.

When strong sun reflects off buildings – especially white-painted Mediterranean-style buildings – you're getting a double dose. Likewise, you're especially vulnerable sitting round a pool. The water and the concrete surround both reflect the sun's rays.

Sunburn is not uncommon on skiing holidays. Even if you feel cool up a mountain, the sun blazing through the clear, thin atmosphere and reflecting off the snow can be dangerous. The thinner the air, the stronger the rays.

When you do burn: If you ignore all this killjoy advice, and you can't resist that extra half-hour in the sun, the results can be agonising. But don't let it spoil your holiday. There are some helpful remedies.

- Use calamine lotion to cool and soothe heat rash and sunburn. Believe it or not, yoghurt is very good too – I recommend plain not fruit flavours.
- To soothe a raging skin, pour two pints of strong tea into a bath of tepid water and soak in it.
- At night put gauze over your calamine lotion or yoghurt dressing, to stop you sticking to the bedsheets.
- Use plenty of moisturising cream to stop your skin from drying out. One dermatologist claims that massaging Vaseline into your face is as effective a way to put off wrinkling as any expensive moisturiser or after-sun cream.

The safest tan of all: Use false tan for the safest colour, to enhance a light tan and to brown sore pink flesh. Before you apply false colour, moisturise your skin first. Put on the 'colour' with a damp sponge. The colour will be deepest on dry hard skin, so apply it very lightly on elbows and knees.

I prefer the products that are already coloured brown so that you can see where you're putting it. Always wash your hands after applying the cream and don't sleep in your best white sheets. If you sweat in the night you'll stain them an unpleasant streaky brown.

A cheap alternative for a short-term pale fake tan is to cover your skin in cold strong tea or coffee (without milk).

No kind of false tan gives you any protection at all from the sun's rays.

Handling the heat: Even if you avoid the worst of the sun, hot weather by itself can be a health risk to those who aren't used to it. Some of the more unpleasant effects are prickly heat, dehydration and heat exhaustion.

When your sweat ducts are blocked so that sweat cannot escape and evaporate, a rash develops which can itch intensely – prickly heat. To help avoid it, wash your skin before you apply a second coat of suntan cream, and wear loose clothes. Use talcum powder to soothe.

Too much sun, especially if you're rushing around in it, can cause headaches and nausea. You need to drink a lot of fluids, and regularly. If someone is noticeably ill, put them in a cool room on a wet sheet. Keep sponging them and make sure they drink some fluid with salts. Get medical help. You don't need to be up the Amazon to suffer from heat exhaustion.

Dehydration – loss of water from your body – can be serious, especially in children. Alcohol has a dehydrating effect, even in cool climates, so go easy when it's hot. To overcome dehydration, you need to drink plenty of non-alcoholic drinks, and also replace the salt that's lost through sweat. Mix up this recipe and take it as often as you can:

8 level teaspoons of sugar or honey
half a level teaspoon of salt

1 litre of clean water
optional: a squeeze of orange or lemon juice for flavour.

A rehydrating mixture shouldn't taste saltier than tears.

- Gulping ice-cold drinks in very hot weather causes stomach cramps. Why do you think that the locals in places like India and the Far East drink tea in the heat?
- Loose clothes and natural fabrics are more comfortable and make you sweat less than tight clothes and man-made fabrics.
- Breastfeeding in the heat can make both of you hot and sticky. Put a thin towel or cotton scarf between your flesh and baby's.

• Photographs

This One's a Bit Dark But You Can Just Make Out Auntie's Feet

For most of us, taking photographs on holiday is all part of the great holiday experience. Mind you, some people seem to take them more from a sense of duty than for pleasure, while for others they simply make lovely souvenirs, graphic reminders of some of the best times of the year.

Some people get so involved with taking their photographs, you wonder whether they ever look at the sights for real or whether they only ever see them through a viewfinder. I was once in a church in Rome looking at a famous painting. While I was staring at it, a young Japanese girl came up to the side-chapel with her nose in a guide book. She lifted up her camera and photographed the picture, then she turned to a vending machine on the wall and bought a postcard of the painting. Then she left. She never once looked at the thing with her own eyes.

You don't have to have an expensive camera and a bag of lenses to take good photographs. Certainly, having a modern fancy camera is no guarantee of good shots. Here are some sensible tips for those of us who are not photography buffs but do like taking photographs of our travels. (Some of them also apply if you own a video camera or are planning to hire one for your holiday.)

Film speeds: The 'speed' of a film measures how sensitive to light it is. The faster the film, the less light you need to take a reasonable photograph. For colour-print films, ISO 100 and 200 are medium speeds. ISO 400 and the fairly new ISO 1000 are fast films. With a fast film you can carry on taking pictures longer without flash at dusk when the light starts going.

With faster film, you can also 'freeze' moving subjects better, by using a faster shutter speed, if you can adjust this on your camera – or a fully automatic compact camera will use a fast shutter speed automatically.

Use transparency film if you hope to get your pictures published, or if you're prepared to set them up in a carousel for slide shows. Otherwise, colour prints are more convenient for showing round when you get home.

Buying film: Unless you're going to America or Japan, you're usually better off buying your film at home before you leave. In some countries film is much more expensive and there may be a limited choice of types. Sometimes the film on sale is past its sell-by date, and sometimes it has been stored in the heat which ruins it.

Don't rely on getting films at the airport as you fly out. They might be out of stock of the sort you need. Film on sale at British duty-free shops is no cheaper than at ordinary shops.

Care for film: You can damage film if you keep it in high temperatures. Professionals keep theirs in a fridge whenever possible. Don't leave your camera with a film in it on the back shelf or seat of a car in hot weather. Don't leave it for long in a window under the full glare of the sun. Remove a film from the camera as soon as it's finished, and put it in a cool dark place.

Processing: Unless you're staying in a sophisticated country and you desperately want to see your pictures, wait until you get home before you have your film developed.

Batteries: Put a new battery (or batteries) in your camera before you leave home, and take spares with you. Even in countries which sell the right battery for your camera, you can lose precious holiday time looking for the right shop. If you're taking a separate flash unit, take plenty of batteries for that, too.

Airport X-rays: Whatever they say, the X-ray machines at airport security checks *do* affect film, whether it has been exposed or it's still in the packet. (The effect is a slight 'fogging', like a hazy overexposure of the photographs.)

True, the machines at British airports deliver a very mild dose, which doesn't affect medium-speed film noticeably. But in other parts of the world, especially in underdeveloped countries, a fiercer dose of X-rays can do more damage. Fast films are more sensitive, too. And in any case, there is a cumulative effect – so if you'll be going through several airport security checks on your travels, your film is at risk. The best answer is to try to avoid sending film in a bag down the X-ray conveyor belt. There are three possible alternatives.

First, you can pack all your film in a case that's being checked in to travel in the hold. But these days, for security reasons, this is sometimes X-rayed too.

Secondly, you can ask politely for your film to be hand-searched by the security people. Keep it in a see-through plastic bag at the top of your hand luggage so that you can get at it easily. They're not obliged to examine it by hand, but at British airports they usually will. Abroad you may find they won't co-operate.

Finally, you can carry all your film about your person in pockets. The arch you walk through at the security desk is a metal detector which doesn't affect film.

Protect your camera: Don't let dust and sand blow into your camera. When you're not using it, keep it in its case or well wrapped in a polythene bag. If you're photographing in a dusty place, clean the camera with a soft brush at the end of every day.

Cameras and seawater don't mix. If you drop your camera in the sea, it will be ruined beyond repair. Even salt spray should be wiped off immediately.

Make sure you travel with an insurance policy that will cover the cost of a similar new camera.

Duty paid: If you're taking new camera equipment abroad with you, stick the receipts in your wallet. Then, if you're stopped at customs on the journey home, you can prove that you didn't buy the camera abroad or in a duty-free shop.

Avoiding unhappy snaps

- The most interesting snaps are those of people doing things, not standing stiffly in front of the camera.
- When you photograph a famous sight or landmark, use people in the foreground to give a sense of scale.
- In sunny weather, the middle of the day is the worst time for photography. The light is harsh and the shadows short and strong. In early morning and late afternoon, you'll get softer colours and more interesting shadows.
- Try creating a 'frame within a frame'. Shoot the picture through an archway or with an overhanging branch round the top of the picture for a natural frame.
- Avoid shaky pictures. Take a deep breath and hold it just before you take a picture. Squeeze the shutter, don't jab at it. If possible, rest the camera on a wall or something firm while you shoot.
- Study postcards and picture guidebooks for ideas of where to shoot the most interesting scenes.
- At famous landmarks that everyone knows about, take photographs from an unusual angle or level. Just crouching down or standing up on a wall can make a snap more interesting than one you shoot at normal eye-level.
- When you photograph open countryside or the sea, you generally need something of interest in the foreground to stop it being boring.
- For an unusual effect, try using flash in broad daylight. The experts call this 'fill-in' flash. If you are photographing someone in the shade, say under a tree, the flash will light up their face.
- If you plan to put your holiday prints in a album, photograph signposts and maybe your hotel sign and use them instead of writing a title on the first page.

Extra equipment: Why is the shot you take of your holiday beach quite unlike the photograph in the holiday brochure? Because the professional photographer will have used at least one filter on his camera. If your camera is the sort that will take a filter (for instance a 35mm SLR), you should at least keep an ultra-violet filter fitted at all times. As well as reducing the hazy effect of a bright sunny day, it also protects the lens from damage.

Then you should consider using a polarising filter, which reduces reflections from water and glass, and adds colour to a bright sky. And possibly also a warm filter (like an 81A) to add colour to a scene that's 'bleached out' by strong sunlight.

Another useful accessory when you're photographing in sunny conditions is a lens shade (or lens hood), which keeps the sun from shining into the lens and causing flare. Without one, you can shade your lens by holding your hand or a magazine horizontally above and in front of the camera. You can see the difference it makes through the viewfinder.

Security: In most countries it is very unwise to photograph 'sensitive' areas such as army barracks, airports, soldiers and sometimes even bridges. You may be arrested as a spy. At airports always first ask an official or someone in uniform for permission to take a snapshot. If it is refused, put your camera away.

Photographing people: We have no moral right to photograph local people just because we think they might make a good photograph. Quite understandably, some people get annoyed by this. Others are offended. Wherever possible, ask for permission first and respect the wishes of anyone who says no. In St Lucia the locals hate being photographed and can get very angry if you point a camera at them. I heard one traveller ask a guide in a hushed voice, 'Is this because they think we are snatching their souls?' The answer is that the St Lucians simply feel they are being exploited by the cameras and they hate it.

In some tourist areas, local characters will expect to be paid and you should honour this with the going rate. In

Morocco, for instance, you'll find it difficult to photograph street performers and musicians unless you have a handful of small change. They've worked out exactly how much they expect for one picture. Video recordings come extra.

If you really want to capture the locals going about their daily business, invest in a telephoto lens and use it discreetly from a distance. For the occasional, not-to-be-missed shot, you can ask a friend to pretend to pose near for you. Point the camera in their general direction but actually focus it on your unwitting subject.

If you promise to send a print to anyone you have photographed, do please honour your promise. If you don't, you'll just make people distrust photographers more than ever.

And finally: When you get your slides or prints back, make the effort to label them. Hands up all those of us with a drawer full of snaps of people and places we can no longer put a name or date to.

• Holiday Temptations

Holidays are a time for spending money – and so they should be. Penny-pinchers make dull holidaymakers. You won't relax and enjoy your time if you're constantly counting the cost of every little luxury. Sometimes it's the little extras that make all the difference between a good holiday and a great one – take a taxi instead of a bus . . . go to that smart restaurant that looks really good, not the grotty one that's a bit cheaper . . . if you fancy a bottle of Champagne instead of the cheap plonk for a change, why not?

When you add up the cost of those little treats, they probably don't amount to much compared to the full cost of the holiday. But even so, there are some temptations to beware of. Sometimes on holiday you're invited to spend money on things you just don't encounter at home. And that's where you have to watch out that yielding to temptation isn't going to cost you a packet.

Excursions: I asked some holiday reps why they never passed on all their useful information about the local banks, the market days, shopping hours, undrinkable water, etc. during the long coach ride from the airport to the resort. Why did they keep it all back for the welcome meeting the next morning? 'If we told them everything on the bus,' they said, 'no one would come to the welcome party and then we'd never sell them any excursions and we'd lose out on a lot of cash.'

Most holiday reps earn a commission on the excursions they sell to their clients. This doesn't necessarily mean that every trip is a rip-off. Far from it. You just need to be on the alert before you sign away all your traveller's cheques.

Before you sign up for any organised trip, talk to holidaymakers who are in the middle of their fortnight's stay. They may already have tried some of the trips and can give you a first-hand opinion of them. They will also be wise to how well the local transport works and how much it costs. Many a £10 half-day trip to a local market costs under £1 if you use local buses.

Some excursions can be cheaper and more fun if you organise them yourself. When you visit a place under your own steam you please yourself about how much time you spend on your visit. It's galling to have to rush around a place you really like, to catch the excursion coach back. Equally, there's nothing worse than being stuck somewhere you *don't* find interesting and having to kill time until the coach takes you home.

Far-away holidays: Be especially careful after a long journey. After a long flight through different time-zones your brain doesn't function as sharply as usual. Business people are always being advised not to make important decisions for the first twenty-four hours of any trip a long way from home because of the effects of jet-lag. Holidaymakers should heed the advice, too, and avoid signing up for expensive extras (or making any sort of major financial transaction) for the first day or two of the holiday.

However, you can often be put under pressure to buy trips at the welcome meeting on the day you arrive. Therefore some time before you leave home, ask the holiday company to provide you with a list of the optional excursions (and their prices) that they will be offering you when you arrive. Then you can look up the places and read about them in guidebooks and give yourself a clear idea, before you arrive, of the trips that you might want to buy.

Shopping: Holiday reps invariably set up deals with local shopkeepers, restaurant owners and nightclub managers. In return for recommending their clients to these places, the holiday rep will get free meals and drinks and, from the shopkeepers, commission or free goods. Again, this doesn't mean that any places that are recommended to you are not worth visiting. Just don't let any gushing sales talk from a holiday rep cloud your own judgement.

To tip or not to tip? The more expensive the hotel, the more you'll be expected to tip. Many travellers generously tip a head waiter at the *beginning* of their holiday to make sure that they'll get good service during their stay.

If you want to tip the person who has been cleaning your hotel room every day during your stay, hand the money to the cleaner in person. If you leave the money on the dressing table you can't guarantee who will get it. A colleague left some well deserved cash for the chambermaid in her room just before she checked out (and some hours before the maids came back on duty). She went downstairs to reception to pay her bill leaving the porters to go up and bring her case down. Just seconds after her case had been collected she went back to her room to pick up a coat she'd accidentally left in the wardrobe. The money had gone.

In countries where Western products are very hard to come by and very expensive, do think of leaving any unused soap, tights or toiletries you brought with you as a farewell thank-you.

If you pay for a meal with a credit or charge card, and you add your tip to the total before you sign the voucher, there's little chance that your waiter will receive his cut. If you want your tip to go to the staff who served you, and not the management, it's more likely to happen if you leave a tip in cash on the table.

The credit card scam: When you pay by credit card, beware the restaurant that leaves the bottom line on the voucher – the one for the total bill – blank, even though the bill includes service. They're hoping that you'll forget that the total includes their service charge and that you'll add on another ten per cent or so before you sign.

Telephone temptations: Hotels with telephones in the bedroom and direct dialling systems whack on a hefty mark-up for each call you make. You may not always want to trek out to (and no doubt queue for) an international phone box. To stop yourself running up a shocking bill for the phone in your room, set a limit on how much you want to spend on a long-distance phone call and ask the hotel receptionist to interrupt you when you reach your limit.

Set em up, Joe: Be wary of running up a high hotel bill for drinks, snacks and extras. Pay as you drink is the simplest way of avoiding a nasty shock as you check out. Otherwise, make a note of what you're spending every night so you'll know how your bill is mounting up.

Timeshare temptations: Some timeshare owners are happy with the deal they've bought. Some are not. Some timeshare companies are reputable. Some are not. Many of them employ hard-sell tactics and in a lot of holiday resorts you'll find it impossible to stroll around the town or along the front without salespeople, hungry for commission, hustling you to view the property they're desperate to sell.

You can be offered all sorts of 'free gifts' to tempt you along to view – and although the sales talk usually includes the line, 'There'll be no obligation to buy', you can find yourself at the receiving end of some very smooth sales talk once you get to the place.

If you choose to visit a timeshare property or go to a timeshare 'party', don't take any credit cards or traveller's cheques with you. This way there's no way you can be sweet-talked into putting down a deposit. All you can do is offer to contact the company another day. This gives you time to review the idea of signing up in your own time.

Don't believe the line about qualifying for a special offer price if you sign up there and then. It'll be a deal that is offered to every potential buyer every day.

If they show you charts and figures that 'prove' how much money you can save on holidays by buying into a timeshare scheme, ask for a copy of the figures that you can study in your own good time.

If you're considering buying into a scheme, ask for any

promises that the sales person makes to be put in writing before you sign.

Buying timeshare accommodation means that you buy the right to spend a certain week or weeks there every year for a fixed number of years. These weeks can be leasehold or freehold, and can be rented out, sold, bequeathed or exchanged.

It is unwise to buy a timeshare deal on the spur of the moment when you're on holiday. If the general idea appeals to you, before you travel away, consider the following points:

- Can you afford to buy?
- Do you want to return to the same place every year?
- Will you always be able to take your holiday during the same week(s) every year? Will you want to?

When you have a particular place in mind to buy, ask yourself:

- Is the area and the resort right for you and the family?
- Will it still be your sort of place in, say, 15 years' time?
- Who owns and manages the place and who will own and manage it when every week is sold?
- Is there a well-established Owners' Committee?
- How much control do time-owners have in maintaining standards?
- Do the charges cover long-term building maintenance as well as cleaning, gardening, replacement and refurbishment?
- Is there an internal exchange system so that you can swap the weeks you visit with another time-owner in the same development?
- If the development belongs to Resorts Condominium International (RCI) or Interval International (II), you can then swap your share for a stay somewhere else.
- Will you be able to sell your share back and, if so, for how much?
- If the sales person is putting heavy pressure on you

to buy, ask yourself why. What's wrong with the place?

Before you sign, check that you are being offered a 'cooling-off period' of at least five days, during which you can change your mind. If you do change your mind, will you be charged a cancellation fee – 'to cover the administration' – and how much will it be?

Timeshare holidays are not free holidays. You still have to pay the cost of getting to your accommodation, and of supporting yourself while you're there.

Some British timeshare companies belong to the Timeshare Developers Association which offers guidelines to anyone thinking of buying into a timeshare holiday home. Like ABTA and package holidays, the TDA is in the business of selling its members products but it does offer advice about dealing with the dodgier practices (of non-members) in the business. TDA, 23 Buckingham Gate, London SW1E 6LB.

• Africa

NORTH AFRICA

This is the part of the world for sights straight out of *The Arabian Nights'* – deserts, palm trees, camels, Arabs in flowing robes. And it can be conveniently coupled with European-style holiday hotels and always plenty of hot sun.

Egypt, Morocco and Tunisia are the three top tourist countries of the area. In all of them you can pick up exotic souvenirs – although the haggling for them may wear you out – and less exotic stomach bugs which *will* wear you out.

As in all Moslem countries, women have to be particularly careful to observe social customs. For instance, topless sunbathing is just not on, except sometimes round hotel pools and on hotel beaches where the guests are European and the staff are worldly-wise. The rule is: stay covered if everyone else is.

Out and about, the wise female tourist covers at least the top half of her arms, and her legs at least down to her knees. The most sensible outfit is lightweight loose trousers and a top that shows little flesh. As well as keeping you cool, this will save you tedious hassles and earn you respect. In my experience, when you're haggling over prices, the more flesh a woman flaunts, the less seriously she is taken and the higher the prices.

Another tip, for both sexes, when in the Arab world: if you eat anything with your fingers, use only your right hand. Eating from your left hand is deemed to be pretty disgusting and barbaric. (Traditionally people use water and not toilet paper to clean themselves when they've been to the loo. You use your left hand for that and eat with your right.)

EGYPT

Egypt offers some of the most famous and stupendous ancient sights on our planet. They are so impressive that even the tourist crowds, the constant hassle of locals on the make, the heat and dust and the tiring sightseeing schedules don't spoil their impact.

Money: Egypt's a country where no transaction is ever straightforward. You won't need to learn much of the local language (English is widely understood) but you will know the word *baksheesh*, from the minute the first unofficial 'porter' fights to the front of the crowd to carry your bag.

The word can be translated either as 'tip' or simply as 'hand-out'. You can't move in Egypt without being asked for *baksheesh*. Even if your tour is supposed to be inclusive, you will constantly need a pocketful of small change for porters, drivers and guides. If someone quibbles over how much you've handed over and you don't think he deserves more, stand there stony-faced and silent. If you start an argument it will be long and loud and draw a crowd. Don't expect other Egyptians to side with you.

Shopping: Don't buy anything on your first day, or from the first salesman you meet. It will take you at least two days to get into the swing of bargaining and knowing the average realistic prices. You'll find that the conversation over dinner is more often about who paid how much for what than about the finer points of the Pyramids.

Food and drink: Don't, don't *ever* drink the water. Don't eat salads that have been washed in water. And don't ever take ice-cubes in your drink – freezing the local water doesn't kill the bugs. It was on my first trip to Egypt that I picked up something from the water that made me ill for a year. It says a lot about the appeal of the country that I did return. On my second trip, the Australian tour rep made fun about me being so particular – until he was horribly struck for two days with sickness and the runs. I wasn't. Ah, the Pharaoh's revenge.

Alcohol is expensive, so bring in your own duty-frees. You're allowed to import one litre of spirits per adult. I find Egyptian wine undrinkable. Cairo is the only place in the world where I have seen journalists refuse a free bottle of wine and ask for mineral water instead. Many of the Egyptian restaurants are unlicensed.

Passionate pests: If you're female and single, wear a wedding ring. This helps stop the endless unwanted overtures from Egyptian men who have quite a thing about us European women. In Egypt I not only invent a fictitious husband, I make sure pursuers are told that he is Egyptian, he is an army captain and we have five children, all boys. That shuts them up.

Sightseeing: The sights to see in Egypt are stunning. But seeing them is exhausting. Most tours start very early in the morning, before the intense heat of the day. You'll need firm walking shoes for the dusty, uneven ground and a hat for shade. A foldable paper fan will come in useful, and so will polythene bags to protect your camera from the dust and sand, and a shoulder-bag for carrying a bottle of water with you.

Take a torch with you. You'll need it when you visit the tombs. Lighting inside the tombs and pyramids is not very good and there are often power failures – a claustrophobic's nightmare, quite honestly, but the sights are worth it.

What to take: Pack all the toiletries and medicines you might need and all your film and batteries. You can buy film in Egypt but it's expensive and may be out of date or ruined by being stored in the heat.

When to go: Winter is the most pleasant time to visit Egypt: the climate is warm and dry from October to May. As a result, that's also the most crowded and most expensive season for tourists. Egyptian summers are stiflingly, almost unbearably, hot.

MOROCCO

You can visit Morocco for winter sun in the organised internationalised beach resort of Agadir. Marrakesh offers the classic 'fascinating blend of the old and new', with well run Westernised hotels and a city centre that hasn't changed much since the Middle Ages. Only the snake-charmers in the main square have tweaked up their act for the tourists.

Driving round the country isn't difficult – the main roads are well kept and pretty empty. There are impressive historical sights to see.

Language: French is the second language after Arabic. Hotel staff speak English and most stallholders and shopkeepers speak a little. You'll get by better with French.

Unofficial guides: In places popular with tourists, like Marrakesh, you can't leave your hotel on foot without men and boys pestering you to let them be your guide. If you're not on a group guided tour, you have to be very firm and purposeful for the pesterers to leave you alone. However, if you're pushed for time, you might be glad of a local to take you round the *souk* (market) and the *kasbah* (palace) – they are easy places to get lost in. But if you have no schedule to keep you will eventually find your bearings.

A 'guide' will inevitably take you to the shops and stalls of his family and friends, or merchants who will pay him a commission on what you buy. If you accept a 'guide' fix the fee first.

Photographs: Ten years ago when I tried to take some pictures in the main square at Marrakesh, the people I wanted to photograph threw stones at me. In 1989 they just demanded money. Photographers these days only get by with a large pocketful of coins.

TUNISIA

Tunisia has a well-developed tourist industry. The sandy beaches at the popular package holiday resorts are lined with low-rise holiday hotels, which offer the swimming pools, dining rooms, souvenir shops and entertainment we expect in established, popular holiday places. Some guests don't ever leave the hotels. Others choose Southern Tunisia for its desert and beautiful oases.

Language: French can be useful. Many Tunisians speak French as well as Arabic. The staff in the holiday hotels can speak English.

Money: Keep the receipts you get when you change money. You're not allowed to take dinars out of the country, and when you come to leave Tunisia you can only change back into sterling one-third the total amount you've changed. Take small denomination traveller's cheques, so that you're not stuck with large quantities of dinars. When you're haggling over prices in the markets, you'll be expected to pay cash.

Drinks: Imported spirits are expensive. Take in your duty-free. There are well priced duty-free shops you can visit at Tunis and Monastir airports *as you arrive* as well as when you leave.

Local wines and beers are much cheaper than imported ones. Tunisian wine is fine to drink and costs around £3 a bottle. If you like wine, order a bottle from the hotel bar rather than a round of cocktails – it'll cost you a lot less.

The Tunisian spirit is called *boukha* and is made from figs. It's one of those fiery drinks that seems OK when you're on holiday – you can dilute it with mixers – but in my experience the bottle you bring home as a souvenir gets opened once and then sits at the back of the sideboard for ever, gathering dust. Without palm trees, desert sands and sizzling heat, it's best left for lighting the barbecue.

Tips: People don't hang around so aggressively waiting for tips as they do in Egypt. Staff at the top international hotels expect tips; less so at the ordinary holiday hotels. At the airports the porters, if you use them, make a set charge per bag.

Shopping: In the markets, you're expected to haggle but

it can be reasonably friendly barter and less aggressive than other North African countries.

Passionate pests: European women, especially blondes, are considered fair game. Expect to be pestered especially if you flaunt a lot of uncovered flesh.

Inconvenient: Avoid the loos in the local bars. They are pretty unpleasant. Dive into the nearest hotel instead.

Cars: Car hire is not cheap but driving around isn't difficult. Don't ever head off into the desert without taking specialist provisions and advice on where to go and what to do should you break down.

THE GAMBIA

The most popular package holiday destination in West Africa is The Gambia. The travel industry sells it as the place for winter sun holidays with a difference – the tourist season runs from October to May. This tiny country is a wonderful find if you want to experience Africa in the raw. It's not so brilliant if you're just after a change of scenery from the Canaries and for you shopping malls and masses of night-life are a holiday necessity.

Duty-free: No need to take duty-free booze into The Gambia. You can buy just about every liqueur and spirit and a good selection of French wines in the supermarket in Bakau (close to most of the hotels). All at duty-free prices.

Newspapers: When you land in The Gambia, don't leave your newspapers on the plane. You can't buy them in the country and, as you queue for customs, you'll find the local porters and the homeward-bound holidaymakers all begging for your papers. If you don't hand them over at the airport, take them to your hotel and give them to your chambermaid or other guests.

Necessities: The Gambia is a poor country, with very few European-style shops. There are many things you simply can't buy there. Take with you all the toiletries, suntan creams, books, batteries and medicines that you might need.

Binoculars: If you're at all interested in wildlife, especially birds, take some binoculars. There are no 'big game' animals left in The Gambia, but you'll see crocodiles, monkeys and a dazzling variety of tropical birds, from bee-eaters to vultures.

Hazy days: It can be cloudy in The Gambia during the holiday season. It will still be hot but you might not capture many blue skies in your photographs. Don't be fooled: you can still get sunburnt through the haze.

Gambian friends: Outside, the hotels, the local lads hang around waiting to strike up conversation with the tourists. They offer to be your 'friend' and show you around.

I don't know of any tourists who have been ripped off by these fellas. They just want to practise their English, show off their country and earn a few bob by being your guide. If you don't want their company you have to say so firmly and politely. Telling them that you already have a Gambian 'friend' can help persuade them to leave you alone.

Postcard presents: Some of the lads know how much tourists enjoy glimpsing a little 'real life' and they may invite you back to their home. This is the time to bring out your collection of snapshots from home and give away postcards of international pop stars, footballers, the Royal Family, and snow scenes.

Pen friends: Schoolchildren all over the country beg for pens. If you visit a school you'll see just how desperately short of equipment the schools are. Take a few packs of ballpoints with you. If you're on a day's outing in an open truck, never just throw the pens at the children running after you. A child has been blinded by a thoughtlessly thrown pen.

Photographs: You won't be able to buy film anywhere in The Gambia. Take as much as you need. There's nowhere in the country to have film developed, either. That's why photographs are such a coveted status symbol.

If you have a camera you'll find that you're besieged by children asking you to photograph them. They then hand a scrap of cardboard with their address (usually care of their school) and ask you to send a print. It's very tempting to shoot away and then once you're back home you never get around to posting off the pictures.

I was walking once through Banjul, the capital, with some Gambian schoolboys we'd befriended. A mate of theirs came rushing up, eyes shining with joy, with a large envelope he'd just received. Inside were some large prints of him and his family that had been taken by a couple on holiday from Streatham. I watched everyone in the street stop and crowd round. The lad was so chuffed with the pictures I vowed always to keep any promises I made about forwarding photographs. I also found that a polite 'No, I'm sorry. I can't take your photograph. I won't be able to send it to you' was met with understanding and a smile. No harm done. A Polaroid camera must surely be an instant hit.

Tipping: The Gambian lads who act as guides will expect some money at the end of a tour. Many of them are too meek to hassle you badly for it but you'd be pretty mean not to give them a couple of pounds at least for their time.

You won't be hassled for tips in the hotels or by the taxi drivers, but in such a poor country tips for the cleaners, waiters and drivers are very much appreciated. If you buy an excursion, your holiday rep will suggest that you tip the driver. If he or she doesn't, don't let that stop you.

Shopping: Because the country is so poor, cameras, hip T-shirts, cassette tapes, personal stereos and trainers are coveted like crazy. I once saw a cool dude swanking along wearing headphones. He hadn't got anything to plug them into but he was still the envy of his school gang. Some visitors use their gear to barter for wood carvings and other souvenirs.

There are craft markets on the beaches and roadsides and

beside some hotels. Haggling for a good price is expected. Occasionally you'll see ivory illegally on sale and, just as worrying, turtle shells or bangles made from turtle shell. If every tourist refused to buy these souvenirs, the locals would stop acquiring them to sell and maybe there'd just be a chance of saving these endangered animals from extinction.

'Ebony' souvenirs: You can buy attractive hand-carved statues from the beach and street-market stalls. You may be told that the black carvings are made of ebony. This is unlikely. To find out what they are really made of, rub them hard. You'll probably find that the black shoe polish comes off on your fingers. Canny salesmen will make a show of scratching their black wood (but not too deeply) to show you 'it really is ebony'. True ebony is very heavy and will be more expensive than other woodcarvings.

Getting about: You'll find a taxi rank of sorts outside each hotel. These are pretty well run, usually with an organised queue and a board announcing the rates for most journeys. It's usually best to get the driver to wait for you and then bring you home. You should agree the fare for this before you set off. If for some reason he has to wait an hour or so longer than you agreed you should obviously up his fee.

Religion: The Gambia is officially a Moslem country although, as yet, you don't see many women wearing veils and there are no strict anti-alcohol laws. The country's one brewery produces a decent beer – *Julbrew* – and, would you believe, Guinness and Vimto.

Hotels: All the hotels, with the exception of the posh Kombo Beach, are relaxed about allowing non-residents in – as long as they are tourists and not locals. Use them if you want a drink, a snack or the loo when you are out and about. Locals who are not staff are strictly banned from entering. So the hotels offer welcome relief when you start feeling the strain of constant conversation with boys eager to be your 'friend' and guide.

Airport: The airport has the glorious name of Yundum International. It's as similar to Gatwick as a bottle of Vimto is to Château Mouton Rothschild. When you arrive and climb down the plane steps into the heat, take a few relaxing deep breaths and remind yourself that you are on holiday. There's no point in getting agitated about the chaos that confronts you.

You won't win any points by being near the front of the queue for immigration because you'll still have to hang around for your luggage. When you've retrieved your case through the chaos and confusion, and got it through customs, you'll still have to wait on your tour operator's coach until the last passenger has fought his way through the procedure.

Smart travellers who've been to The Gambia before know to find somewhere to perch just off the runway and admire the birds until the first queue has crowded its way through immigration.

EAST AFRICA

You don't have to be an Attenborough to enjoy an African safari. For most people – me included – a visit to a game reserve is one of the most romantic, exciting and beautiful holiday experiences possible. Of all the African countries where you can have a packaged safari holiday, Kenya is the one that has its tourist industry best organised. It has well run safari camps and lodges which offer more than a touch of the old colonial world. And it has exotic beach resorts on the Indian Ocean into the bargain. Safari holidays to other African countries are generally run by specialist companies, who are good at providing you with detailed information on what to expect. But a lot of my advice on Kenya goes for them, too.

KENYA

Costings: Check that the price of a safari holiday includes the cost of the game drives. If not, you'll need to budget for them.

Alcohol: Take in your duty-free allowance. The local beer is cheap and refreshing, but imported wines and spirits are expensive and locally produced wine is . . . well, let's say it's a bit of a shock to the European palate.

Language: There are more than 40 tribal languages in Kenya. However, your guides and the staff in the hotels and lodges will all speak English. Swahili is a sort of East African Esperanto, a made-up language which enables Africans from different tribes, Europeans and Asians to communicate with each other. It's pretty easy to read and pronounce. You don't need to speak Swahili to get around as a tourist, but it's worth learning a few words from a phrasebook. Swahili-speakers will like you for it.

What to take: Pack a torch. There's not much illumination in most safari camps. Pack a lot of insect repellent – especially if you're visiting the coast – and all the toiletries you might need. You can hire binoculars in Nairobi but it's best to travel out with your own or a borrowed pair.

What to wear: Those khaki safari clothes aren't just a fashion fad. Animals are less likely to spot you and run away if you blend in with the background. Kenya straddles the Equator, so the sun is very strong all year round. However because most of the country is fairly high above sea level, and because you're likely to be up before dawn for game drives, you'll need a warm sweater or jacket. Take a hat to protect your head from the heat, with a brim to shade your eyes from the glare of the sun.

Photography: Take at least twice as much film as you think you'll need. Film in Kenya is expensive and may be old or have been stored in the heat.

The best pictures are shot in the early morning and late afternoon, when the animals are most active. At noon the sun is directly overhead and casts harsh shadows. Fast film is useful on safaris as you are most likely to spot animals at dawn and dusk when the light is poor.

Take a plastic bag to keep the dust out of your camera and its accessories. A zoom or telephoto lens is a must if you want to be able to recognise the animals in your pictures. (If you don't own a zoom or a telephoto, you can hire one from a specialist camera shop before you leave home.)

Safari safety: Always heed the advice of your guide. On safari don't wander off for a walk on your own from your lodge or camp. Quite simply, if you do you could be eaten by a lion or, more likely, trampled to death by a buffalo.

Presents: Children everywhere will ask you – often in quite a shy way – for pens and sweets. Take out some simple ballpoint pens with you – they're worth a lot to the children.

Sweets: The dust and the heat make for dry throats. Take some boiled sweets with you to suck on safari – and take more than you think you'll need. You're bound to want to give some to the children you meet.

Tipping: The staff in the lodges and camps are used to wealthy Americans leaving large tips when they depart. That doesn't mean you have to – at least, they won't be openly resentful if you don't. But it's customary to tip your driver at the end of the safari. If you have a friendly, helpful, well-informed driver, you'll want to anyway.

Nairobi: Don't wander around the streets of the capital at night. During the day, take advice about any possible 'no go' areas – and don't go there. Don't tempt fate and the occasional robber by flaunting your wealth. The public toilets are disgusting. Use the nearest tourist hotel.

On the coast: Resorts like Mombasa and Malindi have a reputation for petty crime – especially theft from tourists. That doesn't mean you're in constant danger of being mugged, but take sensible precautions. Don't stray off the main streets after dark, and don't leave anything valuable unguarded on the beach.

Topless sunbathing in public places is illegal in Kenya – even though you may see local women walking around topless.

• America

Arriving in the USA is like landing slap-bang in the middle of every American movie and television programme you've ever seen. Everything is familiar yet it is all so different.

Visas: The current situation is that to enter the USA you need a full British passport but you don't need a visa *if* you have a return ticket with 'a participating airline'. Find out from your travel agent, the tour operator or the airline themselves whether they qualify. Most of them do.

But you do need a visa to enter the States from Canada by road – so if you plan to take a trip across the border during your stay, you'll need one to get back in. Apply to the American Embassy in London in plenty of time.

If you have an old, expired passport that contains an American visa without an expiry date (an 'indefinite' visa), the visa is still valid, even though you're travelling on a new passport. Take them both with you.

Immigration: Be prepared for long queues at Immigration when you land. The Americans make a great show of being particular about who they let in. If you lose your temper at the seemingly daft questions they ask you, it will take twice as long. The scruffier you look – especially the under twenty-fives – the longer your interrogation is likely to be.

Duty-free: There's not much point in taking alcohol or tobacco over with you to use on holiday. It's easily available at prices comparable to home.

The Americans are hot on not allowing you to import any meat or meat products, seeds, plants or fruit. Once when I landed in New York with an orange left over from my in-flight picnic, it was confiscated with much ceremony.

The cost of a holiday: When you're working out your budget, bear in mind that most package holidays to America include only your flight, your hotel room and possibly car hire. A package price rarely includes any meals, not even breakfast.

Hotel prices: If you're booking yourself into hotels, you'll find that many places charge for the room, not the number of people sleeping in it. American beds are wide. A twin room will often have two double beds.

Flash the plastic: America is the home of the credit card and the charge card. If you have any, take them. If you don't, before you leave home, consider applying for one or both of the two free ones – Visa (which includes Barclaycard and others) and Access (which is tied in with Mastercard in America). You'll need a credit card or charge card for picking up a hire car and probably for checking into a hotel.

Changing money: American hotels rarely have money-changing facilities. You need to go to a commercial bank – not a savings or loan bank. These are usually open Monday to Fridays, mornings to early afternoon. But all American banks are surprisingly inefficient. You can also change money at a currency exchange kiosk – you can usually find one in the popular tourist areas.

Traveller's cheques: If you're taking traveller's cheques, take only dollar cheques. In most places you can spend them as you would cash without having to change them at a bank first.

No one wants to know about sterling traveller's cheques – and that includes most banks. I once asked a teller in a Manhattan bank if she could possibly cash a sterling traveller's cheque for me. She replied: 'No way, lady. Not possible. Never. Have a nice day.'

Medical insurance: See the chapter on insurance. America is the big one. Don't dream of going there without an insurance policy that provides huge medical cover – at least £1,000,000. Tourists have been known to have to sell their house to pay for medical treatment they needed in America. Even worse, if you're taken ill or you suffer an accident, without proof that you can pay for treatment, you probably won't even be able to get any.

Muggings: In the big cities you need to be street-wise. If you look like a hesitant tourist you'll be fair game for thieves and muggers. That means never looking as if you're lost, even if this means walking some blocks out of your way. If you do get lost, don't advertise it in the street by looking at the map. Instead head for a quiet corner of a shop or a hotel lobby before you try to find out where you are.

Read page 126 about carrying money safely and remember that street-smart citizens in cities like Miami and New York carry a few ready notes in a pocket as 'mugging money'. They stash their plastic in less obvious places.

Theme parks: Every travel brochure goes overboard describing the joys of Disney World and Disneyland. They never mention the queues. During the school holidays it's best to get there early to avoid the worst of the long lines, and in Florida in summer, to avoid the worst of the humid heat.

Disney World in Florida is less crowded in early June, September, October and for the period between Thanksgiving (the fourth Thursday in November) and the start of the Christmas holidays.

Free car hire? Don't imagine that a 'free car hire' holiday offer means exactly that. The actual hire charge may be waived but you'll probably have to pay for insurance, petrol, collision damage waiver and local sales tax.

Driving: Not everything in America is like the movies. Don't expect to drive fast. There's a national speed limit of 55 m.p.h. In some states, child seats are compulsory for under-fives. You will have to order them in advance and pay to hire them.

Eating out: Don't expect long, late dinners like the ones you linger over by the Mediterranean. Americans eat earlier than Europeans and in many areas the restaurant kitchens close by 9 p.m.

Look out for 'Sunset Special' and 'Earlybird Eater' offers, where restaurants give you a discount for eating before the main evening rush.

The 'happy hour' was invented in the USA. Some bars not only sell drinks cheaper in the early evening, they offer free snacks as well.

In some states, restaurants are obliged to add a sales tax to the bill – but they don't usually bother to mention that on the menu.

Coffee can be surprisingly weak but in most places you can drink as much as you like for the one price.

Tipping: If you've ever watched American tourists in Europe, you'll have noticed that they tip just about everyone they come into contact with. And in the States the cab-drivers, waiters, porters and doormen – just about everyone except shop assistants – will expect you to tip them.

Waiting on tables is an art form in America. 'Hi. My name is Joe and I'm your waiter for the evening. Now, how can I help you folks have a truly memorable meal?' When Joe is through with his Oscar-winning performances he will expect at least a fifteen per cent tip. If the bill comes with service included, you're not obliged to tip Joe but most diners do.

There's no need to tip anyone in fast-food joints and self-service cafes but some customers leave a few coins on the table.

Manners: On the whole, Americans don't stand on ceremony. After introductions, it's first-name terms all round. Most strangers – your hotel receptionist, cab-driver, waiter, etc. – will greet you with 'Hi! How ya doin'?' It's their equivalent of our more starchy 'How do you do?'

Electricity: Just because Americans don't use kilograms or kilometres, and we sort of share the same language, that doesn't mean that you can use your hairdryer or shaver over there. Not unless it works on 110–120 volts and you have an adaptor plug with two flat pins.

● Australia

Twenty years ago when parents waved goodbye to their emigrating offspring, most of them thought that they'd never see each other again. In those days, even a telephone call to Australia cost half a week's wages. Now the travel industry sells holidays to Australia to people who don't even have any family over there – they're just popping over for a holiday.

True, there are not many of them, yet. Most people who make the trek half-way round the planet have friends and relations they want to see. (In trade jargon, it's called 'VFR' – visiting friends and relations.)

When you think about it, Australia could be the perfect holiday destination for us Brits. The natives are familiar – well, their Ramsey Street certainly is. Half of them speak an understandable English. (The rest speak Greek, Italian, Lebanese or Turkish.) The scenery is varied and can be dramatic. You can drink the water. You can find sun when it's winter in Britain. They even drive on the left.

Health: British short-term visitors to Australia can participate free of charge in their Medicare system, which guarantees free hospital treatment (but not free drugs, dressings or ambulances) and an eighty-five per cent discount on a GP's charges. But you'd still be foolish to travel without full medical insurance.

If illness caused you to miss your flight home, for instance, or you need extra airline seats to accommodate a leg in plaster, you'd have to bear the cost yourself.

Those corks round the hat aren't just for decoration.

They're for keeping the blessed flies and mosquitoes away. The mosquitoes in Australia aren't malarial but they know how to bite. Be prepared for them if you're visiting the hotter, more tropical areas.

There are more cases of skin cancer among white Australians than any other nationality in the world. Worth bearing in mind, even if you are only going to be stretching out on their beaches for two or three weeks. Heed the message of one Australian health campaign which said simply: 'Slip, Slop, Slap'. It means slip on a shirt, slop on some suntan cream and slap on a hat.

Getting around: Don't underestimate the size of the place when you're planning where to go and what to see. Australia is as big as the USA. The flight between Perth and Sydney is as long as between London and Moscow.

Internal flights are expensive. However, there have been schemes where, if you buy your flights around the country before you leave home, you are entitled to a tourist's discount. The same applies to train journeys and to car hire. So it's worth checking with a knowledgeable travel agent when you first plan your trip, to see what special offers there may be.

Tipping: Australians have a reputation as stingy tippers abroad – and that's because they don't go in for it much at home. Cab-drivers, for example, don't expect a tip, although they certainly won't refuse one if you offer it. In many restaurants, there's no service charge added to the bill. Simply leave a tip if you think you've had good service.

Drinks: The beers and wines of Australia are fair dinkum. No need to take your own supplies. If you see a restaurant with the sign BYO, it means it hasn't got a licence. You are invited to Bring Your Own.

Stopovers: Stopovers are a great travel buy. They are a way of breaking up the long flights to and from Australia and having a short holiday in another country. Your choice of places to stopover is dictated by the airline routes. America, Bali, Singapore, Hong Kong and Bangkok are just some of the options. Tour operators and some airlines organise your hotels for you and will get you to and from the airports in your stopover country.

Remember that, however short your stopover is going to be, you may need to organise a visa, inoculations and malaria tablets.

Round-the-world tickets: You might find that the cost of your return journey to Australia is not much less than a special round-the-world air ticket. The name tells you all. Different airlines fly different set routes and you have to name your dates in advance.

A travel agent who specialises in long-distance flights will have more accurate information about the many different routes and prices than an agent who sells mainly European holidays.

Oz facts

- Surprisingly enough, British citizens need a visa to get into Australia. If your travel company doesn't organise it as part of your package, you'll have to apply (in plenty of time) to the Australian High Commission in London, or the consulate in Manchester or Edinburgh.
- Added together, the different Australian states have more public holidays than most other countries.
- Shops close at noon on Saturdays in many towns.
- You'll need a plug adaptor for anything electrical you take. Australian plugs have three flat pins, the kind used only in New Zealand, Papua New Guinea and parts of China. Electricity is 220 volts.
- The quarantine laws are very strict. If you're taking presents for people, don't include food.
- A British driving licence is valid for up to three months. There's no need to get an International Driving Permit.
- Mail can be received anywhere in the country if you have it addressed to Poste Restante, Chief Post Office in the relevant town or city.

• Austria

Most Brits find that Austria is an expensive country. It doesn't belong to the European Community and imported goods accordingly cost more. (Many Austrian goods aren't cheap either.)

Spirits like gin and whisky that aren't made locally are cheaper in the British duty-free shops, so take your own with you. (You're allowed to take in one litre per adult.)

Drinks: Austrian wine has recovered from the anti-freeze scandal of 1985 – at least it has in Austria, though exports are still suffering. Production standards are now very strict and you'll find a wide variety of reliable Austrian wines. Some of them, particularly the sweet dessert wines, are excellent, but none of them are cheap.

When you're eating out, there's no shame in asking for a jug of tap water.

Tipping: Austrians probably have a less relaxed attitude to tipping than the Germans. Even when service is included, most customers eating out round up the change they leave.

Money-savers

- If you stay more than three nights in a hotel in Innsbruck, you qualify for free membership of Club Innsbruck which gives you free rides on local buses. Ask at your hotel.
- Most coach day excursions offered by travel companies are easy to organise on your own and much cheaper. The train system in Austria is good and most towns of interest are small so you don't really

need a guide to show you round in a large party.
Take an up-to-date guidebook instead.

- In Feldkirch near the Austrian-Swiss border, from
April to August there's an open invitation for buskers
to visit and perform. In return you get free bed and
breakfast and around £5 a day – *and* you get to keep
any money you collect in the hat. In early August
there's a festival of buskers with prize money for the
best acts.

• Canada

It's not that many years since just about everyone who visited Canada from Britain was travelling to see friends or relations. Now more than three dozen travel companies offer package holidays to the world's second-largest country and many of us set off not knowing a soul over there.

British passport holders don't need a visa but if you plan to cross the border into the USA during your trip, you'll have to get an American visa before you leave Britain.

Canadian dollars are different from American dollars. You can spend Canadian-dollar traveller's cheques in many shops and restaurants, and many places will also take US-dollar traveller's cheques. You might find places that will take sterling traveller's cheques (unlike in America) but spending is easier with dollar traveller's cheques.

Hotel room rates are based on double occupancy and, unlike some American hotels, you will be charged extra if you squeeze in a third person. Travelling alone is costly because the charge for a single person is very much the same as the double rate.

- Canadians expect to tip as much and as often as Americans. The norm is often a whacking fifteen per cent. Have a nice day.
- Internal flights are expensive. If you expect to fly large distances around Canada, the airlines offer schemes that can save you money. Check out the latest deals with the airlines before you leave home.
- You can drive in Canada for up to three months on a British driving licence. If you plan to borrow a

friend or relative's car while you're there, you should drive with a letter of consent from the car's owner and make sure that you are insured.

- You'll get the best hire car deals if you book through a local company in a Canadian town or city. They usually work out cheaper than when you book in advance with an international firm. However, the local companies are less flexible and you can't drop the car off at a different place from where you picked it up. The most expensive hire cars are those you organise at the airport when you arrive.

- Travel with the highest possible medical cover. As in America, you can bankrupt yourself if you so much as sneeze.

● The Caribbean

Let the sun soak through to your bones and be patient. If the Caribbeans didn't invent the term 'laid back' it was only because they were too relaxed to bother. In the Caribbean, when the electricity goes off, the water fizzles out, the bus never comes, adopt the local way. Shrug your shoulders and smile.

I knew I was finally tuned into the Caribbean style when I ordered a gin and tonic at a swish and expensive hotel bar. I waited and I waited. Eventually the waitress reappeared carrying a beer. 'But I ordered a gin and tonic,' I said. 'Mmm,' she said slowly and thoughtfully, 'but the beer's just as wet.' She wasn't wrong. Cheers.

High times and low times: The Caribbean islands have a definite high season for tourists and a low season. The high season runs from 16 December to 15 April. Hotel rates can jump up 20–40 per cent during this period. However, the weather doesn't change dramatically on these dates, so you can save money by staying the weeks just before or just after the main season. Don't visit in low season – summer and autumn – unless you're prepared to cope with turbulent weather and hair-curling humidity.

The lusher the island, the more it rains. If you hear anyone talking about 'liquid sunshine', they mean rain.

Hotels: Spend time choosing where you are going to stay. Getting around the islands is often expensive and difficult and so you'll be spending a lot of time at your holiday hotel or villa.

Pests: The two worst pests are hustlers and 'No see ums' – flying bugs. Travel with lashings of insect repellent to deal with them (see also pages 116–117), and as for the hustlers, be polite but firm with anyone trying to sell you things you don't want. However much you've had to budget for your holiday, you'll be a lot richer than any stallholder or hustler you see. Keep your sense of humour. They will.

Money: US-dollar traveller's cheques can be more convenient to change than sterling cheques. Many prices are quoted in dollars – but check whether they mean US dollars or the local dollar.

Stripping off: A Caribbean beach is not the place to go to acquire an all-over tan. Women need to be wary about topless sunbathing. It's usually confined to hotel beaches and pools. In many places it is seen as offensive or provocative. On some islands it is against the law.

Photographs: Be wary about photographing local people. St Lucians, for example, hate being photographed. It makes them very angry. Other islanders might ask for money. Have some change ready and maybe also sweets for young children.

You'll take the best photographs in the early morning and late afternoon. The sun at midday is so strong it can bleach out a colour shot.

Tipping: There are certainly no rules *against* tipping in the Caribbean. Check with hotel and restaurant bills whether service has been included. If not, ten per cent is the expected minimum. American tourists usually leave fifteen per cent upwards. The swankier the hotel, the higher the expected tip.

Dress code: The grander (i.e., more expensive) hotels expect men to wear trousers not shorts at dinner, and often a jacket too.

Taxis: Agree the fare before you set off in a taxi. Many taxis don't have meters and those you see don't always work.

Stews: Goat is a popular meat for stews and curries. However, because some sensitive tourists can't bring themselves to eat goat – they see too many kids gambolling along the roadsides – canny chefs often describe dishes as 'lamb'.

• Cyprus

Cyprus, in the Eastern Mediterranean, has been a divided island since the Turkish invasion in 1974. The Turks now occupy the northern third of the island, and the Greeks have the rest.

The Turks call their bit the Turkish Republic of Northern Cyprus – but it's a republic that isn't officially recognised either by Greece or by Britain. Most package holidays are to the southern part of the island, which is mainly Greek in character but with some resorts stuffed with ugly high-rise hotel blocks, discos and restaurants. The tourist industry is only just getting under way in the Turkish-occupied north.

There are many military bases and 'restricted' areas on both sides of the frontier. As the signs forever warn you, in the restricted areas you mustn't stop the car or take photographs. Neither should you use binoculars in these areas to admire the striking scenery.

Greek Cyprus

- Traffic drives on the left (a sure sign that the British once governed a place).
- Buses and shared taxis are cheap.
- The currency is the Cyprus pound which is divided into cents. You can only take in fifty Cyprus pounds but you'll get a better rate anyway if you buy them over there.
- You can use sterling traveller's cheques in many shops and hotels.
- You can only cross the border to the north of the

island at a checkpoint in Nicosia. This can take some time to get through and it isn't always open.

- You won't be allowed into southern Cyprus if you have a north Cyprus stamp in your passport.

Turkish Cyprus

- Because the British government doesn't officially recognise this Turkish republic, the charter airline that flies into the area can technically only issue tickets to Istanbul. You're given the Istanbul-Cyprus part of the ticket on the plane.
- The currency here is the Turkish lire and the exchange fluctuates a little nearly every day. It can pay you to exchange only a little cash, often.
- Traffic drives on the left here, too – but you have to watch out for mainland Turks who bring over their lefthand-drive cars and are prone to forget which side of the road they should be on.
- The cheapest way to travel between the three main towns is by shared taxi. You book a ride at the local *kombos* office.
- As on the mainland of Turkey, you can buy duty-free as you *enter* the country as well as when you leave it. Prices of imported spirits are higher than British duty-free. In the shops and supermarkets local spirits and wines are much cheaper.
- Make sure that the immigration authorities don't stamp your passport when you arrive. With that stamp in it you'll never be allowed into Greek Cyprus or Greece itself. If you ask them, they'll stamp a slip of paper that you carry inside your passport during your stay.
- Holidaymakers cannot visit the south from the north.

● Eastern Europe

You don't take a holiday in an Eastern bloc country to
wallow on paradise beaches or luxuriate in five-star hotels.
Nor do you travel there to bop till you drop to the latest
disco sounds.

Holidays in Eastern Europe are for people who want to
get some sort of first-hand knowledge – however superficial
– of the everyday life in countries very different from our
own. The sights to see can be curious, enchanting and
sometimes dreary. The scenery can be glorious. Hotels can
be grim and the service slow and glum. The bureaucracy
can be frustrating. Conversation with English-speaking
locals may never get beyond football and Michael Jackson.
Or you can find a warmth and interest from locals that
you'll never experience on Costa Concrete beach holidays.

Wherever and however you travel, you'll certainly feel
like a *traveller*, not a tourist – even when you're herded
around on a state-organised tour. You will almost certainly
come home appreciating the many small things in life that
we take for granted. You'll probably also promise never to
moan again at the queues at Tesco's checkout.

Organising your trip: It's much easier to organise the
necessary paperwork if you buy a package holiday and don't
travel as an independent. (Some countries will only let you
in if you are travelling as part of an organised group.)

Leave plenty of time between buying the holiday and
departure for getting the necessary visa. If you have a
'sensitive' job you may find you are refused a visa. Things
are changing fast in Eastern Europe, but until now if you

or a parent were born in an Eastern bloc country, you also need evidence that you have properly renounced your former nationality. The paperwork for this can take some time.

Money: Take sterling traveller's cheques in small denominations issued by one of the major companies. You won't be able to import or export the local currency so it's not wise to change large amounts. Also take sterling and, if you have any, dollars. In many places you can pay with 'hard' currency. But take small denominations. You may pay for something with a £5 note but you'll most certainly be given the change in local currency. In the major tourist areas in some countries you'll find some hotels, restaurants and tourist shops take credit cards.

Keep all the receipts when you change money, and keep any paperwork you're given when you enter the country. You will need to show it when you leave.

Black market: In all Eastern bloc countries black-market currency deals are illegal. In some places you'll find shady characters whispering to you on the street. In others someone you see a lot of, your tour driver, perhaps, or a ski instructor, will offer quiet but open deals. Be very streetwise here. See what other tourists are up to.

Deals with strangers are fraught with danger, not the least of which is arrest and prison. You also leave yourself wide open to being ripped off if you deal with someone you meet in a bar or in the street – with no comeback.

On inclusive package holidays you will probably only need money for souvenir shopping and the occasional 'free time' taxi ride and restaurant bill.

Food: In general, vegetarian and health-conscious dieters fare badly. Many cultures aren't used to vegetarians and if you order a meatless dish you can expect to be served the same stews and soups as everyone else, with the chunks of meat picked out.

Photography: You may feel you look nothing like a spy hero but naïve tourists have been arrested for spying because they pointed their cameras or binoculars towards a 'sensitive' subject. For sensitive, read any military building, anyone in uniform, bridges, planes, airports, tunnels and stations. If in doubt, don't.

If you do get detained or you become involved in an accident or fracas, be very wary of signing any statement that is not written in English (unless you can read the language fluently).

Publications: Be careful with the reading-matter you take into a country. You may find that the newspapers, magazines and books you innocently bought at Heathrow are deemed to be political propaganda. They have equally strong views on immorality. Avoid novels with raunchy covers.

Plugs: Never expect a sink or bath to have a plug. Take a universal plug with you.

Tipping: Tipping customs vary. Most chambermaids and hotel cleaners appreciate presents of anything that is unavailable in the country: new soaps and toiletries, tights. Other people you meet that you might want to tip – your guide and driver, for instance – may well prefer dollars or pounds to the local currency. New T-shirts with English slogans are coveted too.

Duty-free: Take in Western brands of any spirits you want to drink. It's a good idea to take in small bottles to make up the litre you are allowed, rather than one large bottle. You can use them as presents or handsome tips.

ALBANIA

The Albanians are especially hot on confiscating written material they deem to be political or immoral. They will also confiscate any book you try to take in that is about Albania – this page for example!

You can only visit Albania as part of an organised tour. Never turn up late for a group departure. To Albanians, lateness is unthinkable and they will assume you are very ill or feel obliged to send out a search party for you.

Some travel insurance policies exclude Albania. Obviously the one sold by the tour company you travel with won't but check that every other clause in their policy suits you. (See pages 61–65.)

- Theft is unthinkable in Albania. Remember that if you fancy a hotel ashtray as a souvenir.
- Hotel loos are Western in design but Albanian plumbing is . . . interesting and unpredictable.
- At meals you'll probably find bottles of water, beer and wine on the table. You pay for what you drink.
- Pens and chewing-gum make popular presents.
- Beware of jellyfish along the Adriatic coast.

BULGARIA

To say yes, Bulgarians shake their head from side to side. For no, they nod their head up and down. Try it. It's hard to do naturally – and to confuse matters, some Bulgarians who spend a lot of time with tourists know to do it our way. The words to learn are *da* for yes and *ne* for no.

Wine: Bulgarian wine has a good reputation these days. However, some tourist hotels will just serve the rough stuff that doesn't get exported. They decant it into any old bottle.

Skiing: Bulgaria offers low-priced skiing holidays but don't expect state-of-the-art equipment, the highest safety standards or much in the way of *après ski*.

CZECHOSLOVAKIA

- Be especially careful about the books and magazines you bring in.
- If you use taxis and restaurants, round up the bill. Otherwise use tips more to get a service than as a thank-you. To get a table at a restaurant that is 'fully booked', tip the head waiter.
- The US dollar is much more valuable than local currency, and hugely appreciated as a tip.
- Most monuments and churches are only open in the mornings.

EAST GERMANY

When you travel independently into East Germany, even if only for the day from West Berlin, you are obliged to change a certain amount of money which you're not allowed to change back again. This might alter with the social and political changes taking place in this part of the world.

Tipping: Tipping is technically illegal but a ten percent tip is expected from tourists. West German deutschmarks are much more appreciated than local currency. In bars just round up the coins. Nothing untoward will happen if you don't tip.

HUNGARY

Hungarians are big tippers. You'll be expected to tip toilet attendants in return for your ration of paper. If you carry tissues, you'll still be expected to give them the coins. In restaurants twenty per cent tips are the norm. If you pay the bill with a large note you can find that the waiter will assume the extra is all a tip and you won't see any change. To avoid this, and assuming you don't speak the language, write the full amount including your tip on the bill when you pay.

POLAND

You cannot leave the country with more Western currency than you took in (this is to stop you selling coveted Western possessions). You may also be asked to account for what you have spent. Keep all your receipts.

Tipping is not supposed to be encouraged but it is expected. Restaurants usually add a ten per cent service charge. If they haven't, add it yourself. Drivers expect ten per cent.

You should tip the lavatory attendant even if the conveniences are pretty disgusting. Western cigarettes are much appreciated as tips.

Hitch-hiking in Poland is not only safe and legal, it is encouraged by the government. If you plan to travel independently round the country you can buy a book of coupons at the tourist offices in Poland. You use them between May and September and give them to the drivers who pick you up, who can collect them for a prize. Even outside the official hitch-hiking season you shouldn't have any problems finding rides.

ROMANIA

- Waiters expect a five to ten per cent tip even if the bill includes a service charge. Taxi-drivers expect ten per cent.
- Western cigarettes are coveted and some travellers use them as tipping currency.

SOVIET UNION

As *glasnost* gets warmer, the tourist try-ons get stronger. In Moscow, cabs are metered but many drivers, especially if they pick you up from a hotel, refuse to use the meter. You must negotiate the price before you set off. A pack or two of Western cigarettes is often a price they'll settle for. If you pay with cash, use small notes. He may claim he has no change for a large note. Some drivers will demand to be paid in foreign currency.

If the weather is really bad or it's late at night and you can't get a cab to stop for you, hold up two fingers. It means that you're prepared to pay twice the metered fare.

Tipping: Officially, tipping doesn't exist. But that doesn't stop waiters and cab drivers expecting tips from tourists. You can get by with five per cent or some Western cigarettes.

Coffee: Coffee is expensive and of the Turkish sort. You may be grateful for a jar of instant coffee – or it makes a welcome present. You're allowed to take 250 grammes of coffee into the country.

- Bring in any duty-free spirits you might want to drink. You can buy many brands in the tourist shops but at more than British duty-free prices.

- The minimum drinking age is twenty-one.
- Jaywalking is strictly illegal. Only cross a major road at an official crossing or underpass. Tourists have been fined on the spot for not waiting for the green light.
- Public loos can be awful. Try the nearest hotel instead.
- If you don't like hard paper, travel with your own soft toilet tissues.

• The Far East

It doesn't matter how many Chinatowns you've visited in Britain or America, or how many Chinese restaurants you've been to, nothing prepares you properly for the heady shock of visiting the Far East.

The cities are rarely restful. The beaches can be beautiful and – except for the average tourist hotel in China – the hotels are run to a standard that must make European holiday hoteliers weep with jealousy.

The air fare is such a great part of the holiday cost that staying on for another week costs only a small fraction of the total holiday price. Among the brochures you'll find offers of a two-week holiday for the price of one, and three weeks for the price of two. These are arranged with hotels to attract customers in their low seasons when they're not fully booked. The usual condition for the week's 'free' stay is that you pay for half-board – breakfast and one meal a day during that week.

Shopping: Don't assume that everything in the shops is cheaper than here. If you plan to buy cameras, videos, hi-fi equipment, etc., check out the best British prices before you leave home. Remember that you should be paying tax at the customs back home on all your shopping (except the usual allowance of booze, tobacco and scents) over the value of the first £32.

Keep the receipts for the duty and tax you do pay at British customs and travel with it if you take your buys abroad on future holidays. If you do sneak through customs without paying, you'll still be liable to cough up if you're stopped with the item on future trips.

If you overdose on shopping – which is not difficult – you'll find cardboard suitcases and large strong shopping bags cheap and readily available.

If you're planning to buy prints (very tempting in Thailand, Hong Kong and China) take your own stiff tube of cardboard to get them home uncreased.

If you plan to buy any fabrics, it's useful to take out with you a check-list of how much material you need for various items. There's nothing worse than falling for some silk and then back home finding it's four inches too short to make up into the outfit you'd planned.

What to wear: Check out the climate before you book. In Peking, for example, the winters are desperately cold but in July and August there's a heavy humid heat and rain. The annual monsoon doesn't interrupt daily life too much in Bangkok but it rather spoils a beach holiday in Thailand! (Mind you, it's never cold. It's just like sitting on the beach in a hot shower.)

However hot the weather, you'll need a jacket or cover-up for when you are indoors. The air-conditioning can be ridiculously chilly. Many's the time I've shivered in a Hong Kong restaurant and had to open the door to let in some warmth.

Hotels: In Hongkong, Singapore and Bangkok you'll find that the hotels, compared to European ones of similar price, are very good indeed. They work. The ones in the top price-range rank among the very best in the world.

The good news is that you don't have to stay at the posh ones to enjoy their luxury surroundings. It's quite in order for non-residents to visit the bars, restaurants and coffee shops of all the hotels. If you're staying in budget accommodation, you might enjoy wandering into the five-star jobs for a long lingering cocktail or a cup of elegant tea. You'll pay a handsome price for your drink, of course, but unless you're dressed very scruffily you'll be able to linger as long as you like.

CHINA

Since the events of Tian'anmen Square in summer 1989, the Chinese authorities have been desperate for foreign visitors. They need the money and they want to use tourists as propaganda and announce that your presence means that the West must approve of the way the government rules its people.

If you decide to visit China you will find it stimulating, fascinating, occasionally frustrating and always exhausting. You need stamina, tolerance and an open mind.

Although these days some Chinese in the big cities are getting blasé about seeing the visiting round-eyed big-noses, many are still fascinated by our presence. They're also desperate to practise their English and to learn more about life outside their country. You will probably be approached many times by people asking to talk to you. In my experience there is never a hidden sinister motive and you can feel free to talk to them. There is no taboo about talking about religion or politics although this may have changed since June 1989. Here's when some snapshots of your home town and home life come into their own.

Everywhere dress is informal and you shouldn't pack glitzy ostentious clothes. For banquets and business, though, men should wear a suit and tie.

Manners: However much the crowds stare at you, however curt and surly the shop assistant, however gruelling the sightseeing schedule, do not lose your temper. If you have a complaint, try a quiet reasoned word with your guide. Publicly criticising a person is considered the height of cruelty.

Tipping is just not done. If you try to offer a tip, you'll just embarrass and fluster the recipient. However, a small gift of British stamps and postcards, or pretty soap for a woman, is often acceptable if your guide has been very helpful. If he or she refuses to take it, don't insist.

The Chinese are offended and puzzled by unpunctuality. When the guide says meet at three o'clock, you should turn up at three. A colleague of mine once strolled up at quarter-past and the guide was upset and convinced the offender must be ill.

Touching someone is bad manners and can cause offence. Don't pat your guide on the back or link arms with him or her for a photograph.

Hotels: With very few exceptions, accommodation in China is dreary, spartan and smells of mothballs. If you want luxury and obsequious service, stay in Hong Kong.

In the cities, carry a card or letterhead with your hotel's name and address written in Chinese. If you need to get a taxi back you can show it to the driver.

Every hotel room has a thermos of hot water and some tea. If you prefer coffee, take your own jar of instant with dried milk if you drink it white. The Chinese rarely drink milk. You could also pack sachets of any of the 'just add hot water' milky drinks you can buy at home. If you're not happy drinking Chinese tea, which is often quite scented, take your own teabags.

Eating out: I agree with the gourmets who think Chinese cooking is the best in the world. However, the food served up for tourists in Chinese hotels can be *dire*. Look to your guide and any guidebooks you can unearth for recommendations for eating out.

Don't be fazed by chopsticks. Practise in Chinese restaurants before you leave home, because you often won't be given the choice of knives and forks. You don't need to be that deft anyway. The Chinese hold their bowls up to their mouths and use the sticks to shovel the food in. Making a mess on the table is no shame.

Restaurants in China are as overcrowded as the cities. When a place is full, you may find people standing behind your chair waiting for you to finish and move on. Round-eyed tourists are sometimes ushered into a separate room away from the locals. Don't then insist on staying with the locals. You'll embarrass everyone.

Wherever possible go out to eat in a group. The best feasts have many different dishes which everyone shares. This makes a meal for two pretty restricted.

If you're a guest at a formal dinner, it's considered bad manners to take the last piece from a plate. It implies that your host has not provided enough food. Don't start to eat or drink until the host invites you to.

China tips

- Pack all the toiletries, batteries and film you'll need for the trip.
- Don't be tempted to take the ashtray, china mug, chopsticks or whatever as a souvenir from your hotel. Your room-cleaner or the waiter will probably have the cost of the item deducted from their wages.
- Souvenirs can be hard to come by. If you're travelling through Hong Kong, check out the colony's Chinese Arts and Crafts shops, where the best-quality goods are sent straight from China.
- Pickpocketing and theft is very rare. If you are at all at risk, it'll probably be from other visitors.
- If you rent a bicycle to join the hordes of cyclists in the city streets, tie something distinctive round the handlebars so you'll find it again when you park it among the thousands of others.
- Tour groups are sometimes welcomed to an event or a building with applause. The correct and polite reaction is to clap back.

HONG KONG

Hong Kong is an overcrowded but glorious mixture of slick America, quaint 1950s England and the beguiling Orient. The hotels are sophisticated and they work.

Use the Hong Kong Tourist Association (125 Pall Mall, London SW1Y 5EA, tel. 071–930 4775) before you go. They have one of the most efficient set-ups in the world and produce leaflets on all manner of things to do and see in the colony. You can call in to their office in Hong Kong at the Connaught Centre, Connaught Road, Central, tel. 5–244191. (The office, on the thirty-fifth floor, has a spectacular view of the famous harbour.)

Hong Kong is not a place for serious swimming or sunbathing. Hotels don't go in for swimming pools – space is too precious – and they rarely have outdoor sitting areas. There are beaches around parts of the island and on the outlying islands but they're not set up for sun-worshipping. Anyway, everyone is too busy shopping.

Language: Although many people in Hong Kong – especially shopkeepers and hotel staff – speak English, taxi drivers often don't. But they usually know the names and whereabouts of the hotels. If you need a taxi to take you somewhere, ask your hotel receptionist to write the address in Cantonese which you can show the driver.

Crowds: Office-workers have a six-day working week, with only Sundays off. This means that the parks and the ferries to the outlying islands are jam-packed every Sunday. In Hong Kong and China jam-packed takes on a whole new meaning. For a mild and gentle introduction, if you're ever in London, try entering Oxford Circus tube station in the evening rush hour.

Eating out: It's easier to get the full range of authentic Chinese food in Hong Kong than it is in China. You can dine – at a price – in luxurious surroundings in the many swish hotels (whether or not you're staying there). You can queue for the world's cheapest McDonald's. You can fill up on American Club sandwiches and Coke at the coffee shop in every hotel. You can feast in any of the many modest to not-so-modest Chinese restaurants, or you can eat at a rickety table and stool at a pavement or market café. If you can't be bothered with chopsticks, the waiter will find you a spoon and fork.

Shopping: If there's a particular item you are after, let your fingers do the walking. Local phone calls are free (although you may well be charged something if you make them from your hotel room). Use the yellow pages to shop around for the best price. Always tell the shopkeeper you are shopping around – it's amazing how the price can come down.

You can use just about any strong foreign currency and any credit card in Hong Kong. If there was a market value on Green Shield stamps they'd take them, too. Sometimes you can negotiate a better price for cash.

Some shops, especially those selling 'designer' clothes straight from the factory, are not in conventional shopping streets but tucked away in office blocks. The Hong Kong Tourist Office have a list of addresses and opening times.

Hong Kong may still be under British administration (until 1997) but it doesn't count for EC duty-free allowances. When you get home you should pay tax on any goods over your £32 allowance.

SINGAPORE

If you've never been to anywhere in the Far East before, Singapore is a fascinating introduction. If you have, it's a disappointing Westernised version of Hong Kong or Bangkok.

The tiny island state is an interesting stopping-off point on the way to Australia or on the start of a Far East tour, but in itself it's not really worth a week's holiday – unless you enjoy spending all your time in a shopping precinct built of skyscrapers. Most of the traditional Chinese areas have been demolished to make way for modern office blocks – but you can still find superb Chinese food in the restaurants.

Shopping: Like Hong Kong, Singapore is renowned for its duty-free shopping. It's also famous for its rip-offs. If you're buying a camera, for example, be sure you know what the international guarantee looks like. They print authentic-looking fakes in Singapore, to match the fake camera. Similarly, check that the serial numbers on the camera and the lens match. Sometimes old lenses are fitted to new cameras and vice versa.

If the shopkeeper is rude – and Singapore's merchants are famous for their rudeness – remember there are thousands of alternative places to shop.

You can buy from the large duty-free shops *when you arrive* at Singapore airport, not just when you leave from it.

THAILAND

I've met package holidaymakers who talk of their visits to Thailand the same way others talk of their trips to Torremolinos. Certainly the charter flights and the tour operators have made Thailand much more accessible financially. You can visit the country for a holiday on its sugar-white beaches or for a tour of its impressive temples and sights. The best holidays combine both. I've enjoyed my every minute in the country but I know that some holidaymakers find Bangkok a sprawling, polluted, traffic-choked and ugly city.

Manners: It's considered very rude to show the soles of your feet. The foot is considered to be – literally – a very low place inhabited by low spirits. So you shouldn't point your foot at a Thai. Be very careful about crossing your legs and about how you sit on the floor.

The head is considered the most special part of the body because it is believed that your soul dwells there. Avoid touching a Thai anywhere on the head and never pat children on the head.

Buddhist monks take a vow of celibacy and women should avoid touching them or sitting close to them. If a monk accidentally brushes with a woman, he has to undergo a strict act of penance.

If anything goes wrong, on no account lose your temper and scream and shout. This is considered to be very weak behaviour and makes you look foolish in the eyes of the Thais. And once you've lost their respect you most certainly won't get your problem righted. By all means be firm and, if you like, obstinate, but keep cool and calm and always be very polite. As in China, it is considered very insulting if you make someone look foolish by shouting at them.

Always remove your shoes before you enter a Buddhist temple and dress modestly.

Bachelor haunts: In the tourist areas and especially in Bangkok and Pattaya, visiting men are forever being hassled by touts and bar girls who assume that male travellers are visiting Thailand to sample its flourishing sex industry. It's easy and not dangerous for tourists – male and female – to visit the red-light districts just out of curiosity, although you will be pestered to visit the bars and the sex shows. Females who travel around Thailand on their own, find that it's a much easier country than most to visit without being pestered.

• France

When the major holiday companies list the current most popular holiday countries, France never features in the top ten. This is only because the major package holiday companies don't feature France.

Nevertheless, France is one of the all-time favourite holiday destinations for us Brits. We just don't need mass-market aeroplane package holidays to get us there. Most of us drive over in our own cars and head for individually rented places – *gites*, campsites or purpose-built holiday villages. Sometimes we use a company to arrange the accommodation, ferry crossing and some of the paperwork for us. Sometimes we organise the whole shebang ourselves. Either way, there are families who cross the channel every year for their holiday and wouldn't have it any other way.

Language: It's not true that all French people are too pig-headed to speak English to tourists. Maybe some Parisians are too busy to be bothered to stop and chat and be helpful. (Not all Londoners are wonderful, you know.) In rural France, away from the major tourist spots, many French people don't speak English. Why should they? Some school French and/or a pocket dictionary and phrasebook is called for.

August crowds: The French take their holidays *en masse* during August. They jam their roads the weekend of their *grand départ* at the beginning of August and again when they all drive home on the last weekend of the month, *la grande arrivée*. Avoid travelling in France these two weekends.

During August the best campsites and holiday hotels are booked solid, so don't rely on finding anywhere half-way decent to stay if you haven't booked in advance. Many of the good restaurants, especially in Paris, close for the whole of August.

Le shopping: Speciality shops will gift-wrap what you buy free of charge. Make a note of what you buy as you shop so that you won't have to unwrap presents. (But be prepared to unwrap them at customs if you're asked to.)

The further south in France you travel, the longer the shops close for lunch – often a Mediterranean siesta from one to four.

Food shops are often open on Sunday morning. Outside the big cities, shops are often closed Monday mornings or all day Monday.

Weekly street markets and fresh produce markets are often open only in the morning.

Hotels: The price of a hotel room rarely includes the cost of breakfast.

If you're looking for accommodation for the night, never be afraid to ask to see a room before you agree to take it.

Eating out: Don't assume that all meals served in France are award-winning cuisine. They're not. But you don't have to go to an expensive restaurant to eat very well. The French take food seriously, and your best bet is to find out where the local inhabitants eat regularly – not other French visitors and certainly not foreigners.

Don't be afraid to take children and babies to a restaurant. They are welcome in all but the poshest places.

French families like to eat out for Sunday lunch (French women aren't stupid). Book your Sunday lunch well in advance – all the popular places get booked up early.

Meat is served bloodier than in Britain. If you want your meat well cooked you must ask for it *bien cuit* when you order.

Tipping: The French are traditionally great tippers. They tip cinema usherettes and lavatory attendants and expect

loud words to be hurled at them if they don't. In busy
tourist resorts – especially where the British go – it's more
relaxed, probably because they're resigned to the British
who don't automatically think about tipping.

The French leave some coins in the saucer at cafés and,
if you're pleased with the service, you'll be expected to
leave a tip on top of the service charge in a restaurant.
Servis non compris on a bill means that you should add a
service charge of at least ten per cent.

Wine: You can buy good-quality wine at bargain prices
direct from the cellars and châteaux in the wine-growing
districts. Many of them offer free tastings too – so be careful
if you're driving. Don't buy a lot of a locally made wine
until you've been in the area at least a few days and decided
exactly what you like best.

Don't buy wine from roadside stalls where it has been
roasting in the sun all day.

Milk: *Lait cru* is untreated milk usually sold in farm shops.
You must bring it to the boil before you drink it.

Self-catering: Don't expect a teapot or even a kettle in a
French house or apartment. Unless you take your own,
you'll have to brew up using a pan and a coffee pot.

Short change: Beware of being palmed off with a Belgian
ten-franc piece. It's worth pennies. A French ten-franc
piece, which is very similar, is worth around £1.

Daytrips to France: Choose your port carefully. The shortest crossing is to Calais which isn't a very attractive town,
and you have to get a bus from the ferry to the shopping
centre. Boulogne is prettier and you walk off the ferry
straight into the town.

To save time, change your pounds into francs before you
leave home or on the ferry. (You can't change money on a
hovercraft.) Small French restaurants and shops, and some
hypermarkets, don't accept credit cards. Most accept Eurocheques, but they may charge a commission for the
privilege.

Plan an early lunch if you want to experience a good French meal. Most restaurants stop taking orders at two o'clock and tables in the popular places fill up by twelve-thirty.

French carrier bags are usually flimsy. Take your own strong bags or a rucksack. Regular channel-hopping shoppers wheel their own shopping trolleys.

Don't assume all prices are cheaper than home. For major items check your local prices before you set off. Top-of-the-range wines, for example, are no cheaper than in Britain. Packs of local beers and others like Stella Artois and Kronenbourg are. (You're allowed to bring home fifty litres of beer per adult duty-free.)

Don't go over for Christmas shopping on Armistice Day, 11 November. It's a public holiday in France and the shops close.

If you're taking the car over for just a day's shopping, you still need to take your driving licence, vehicle registration book and GB plates. Without a Green Card, you won't have full comprehensive insurance cover in France (see page 73).

Driving: Choose your ferry crossing with your final destination in mind. The longer crossings cost more and there are fewer sailings a day which makes it more awkward if you miss your ferry. However, a longer sail can save on petrol and on the stress of driving.

A holiday route that avoids the busiest main roads is known as a *bison futé* (wily buffalo). Look for the signposts and get a free map showing these routes from petrol stations and information centres.

You're not allowed to drive on sidelights only. You must use headlights. When there's poor visibility during the day, you must drive with two fog-lamps or two dipped headlights.

Visitors don't by law have to have yellow-tinted headlights but the AA strongly recommend that you do. You can buy yellow-tinted beam deflectors. With headlamp converters you have to paint on a special yellow paint – which you strip off with solvent.

When you're buying petrol don't ask for *petrole* which means paraffin. Ask for *essence*, which comes as *normale* (90 octane) and *Super* (98 octane). Unleaded petrol is marked *sans plomb*.

- Children under ten are not allowed to travel in the front of the car (unless it's a two-seater).
- Beware of on-the-spot fines. Pay up but make sure you are given an official receipt.
- Speed limits on all types of road change in wet weather. For example, on motorways the limit is 130 k.p.h. (81 m.p.h.) when it's dry but 110 k.p.h. (68 m.p.h.) when it's wet.
- There's also a *minimum* speed of 80 k.p.h. (50 m.p.h.) for the fast lane of a level stretch of motorway in good daytime visibility.
- If you've held your licence for less than a year, you're not allowed to drive faster than 90 k.p.h. (56 m.p.h.) anywhere.
- If you're planning to use the motorways, you will need plenty of cash to hand. The journey from Calais to Nice using toll roads costs around £35 one-way.

Emergencies: Dial 18 for fire and 17 for police. For ambulance there should be a number written in the phone box. If not, call the police.

• Germany

Beer: Germany's a good country for beer-drinkers to visit. Quite apart from their many beer festivals, the Germans drink more of the stuff than any other nation in Europe. There's a wide range to choose from.

Hell is a lager type and *funkel* is sweeter and made with more malt. *Pils* is light and strong, *Bock* is dark and rich. To order draught beer (*vom Fass*), *ein kleines* is just under half a pint, *ein grosses* is about three-quarters of a pint and *ein Mass* is a litre. Many Germans drink beer with their meals instead of wine.

Tipping: In nearly all restaurants a service charge of ten to twelve and a half per cent is included. In swish restaurants, people leave some coins from their change as a gesture but it's not obligatory, unless of course the service was exceptionally helpful.

Most people don't tip taxi-drivers. Those who do, just round up the fare. You're expected to leave coins in the washroom, even in the loos in garages and restaurants.

German hints

- Take a bathing cap if you intend to swim – they're compulsory in many swimming pools.
- When dining out, ask for tap water unless you specially want the expensive mineral water.
- Shops close on Saturdays around 2 p.m. except for the first Saturday in the month when they stay open all day.
- Tea is expensive to buy in Germany and a packet of

a typically English brand makes a good present to take.

Berlin: You can travel to West Berlin on a British Visitor's passport but if you want to visit East Berlin for the day you will need a full ten-year passport. You may be able to cross the Wall on just a British Visitor's passport – but you will spend nearly the whole day persuading the authorities to give you the necessary visa. Since the recent astonishing changes at the Wall, you may well find that this restriction is lifted. Check the latest situation before you leave home.

• Greece

Many people go to Greece – especially the Greek islands – without booking accommodation in advance. Except at the very busiest time of year (July and August) you can usually just turn up and find somewhere reasonable to stay. If you don't like it after the first night, you can always look around for somewhere else.

It used to be necessary to fly to Athens, then take a ferry to the island of your choice. But now it's possible to fly direct to more and more of the Greek islands. Two words of warning, though. First, the islands with airports are the ones that receive the most package holiday visitors – so if you want to escape the hordes of other Brits, you might need to take a ferry trip anyway.

Secondly, most of the flights to these islands are charter flights – and strictly speaking, you can only travel on a charter if you've booked a holiday that includes accommodation. Greece is one of the countries that are very strict about this technicality. But there is a way round it.

Accommodation vouchers: If you're buying a charter ticket and plan to find your own accommodation, make sure that the airline issues you with an accommodation voucher (it's either free or costs a token £1). Then, in theory, you've bought a package that includes accommodation. You don't need to use the voucher, and the tour companies certainly don't expect you to. But if you turn up in Greece without this bit of paper, during one of their periodic clamp-downs, you could find yourself being charged the full scheduled air fare on arrival or being refused permission to land.

Finding accommodation: You'll find local ladies with rooms to let meet the ferries and buses. Finding somewhere to sleep is only a problem in the major resorts in the busy months of July and August and during the Greek Orthodox Easter.

- Most double rooms in Greece contain single twin beds.
- Greek plumbing is . . . well, very Greek. The basket by the loo is for used toilet paper.
- Sleeping on the beach and camping anywhere other than at official campsites is strictly forbidden.

Duty-free: It's worth bringing in any branded spirit you like (you're allowed 1½ litres duty-free). Locally made spirits are cheaper than well known brands duty-free. Greek brandy is readily available. It's sweeter and cheaper than the French stuff.

Greek wine isn't expensive and you don't have to worry about special vintage years and vineyards. There aren't any. Retsina – or turpentine as many tourists fondly call it – is a taste you can acquire. Ouzo tastes aniseedy and you can dilute it with water.

Easter: Easter for the Greek Orthodox Church can fall at a different date from our Easter. It's a wonderful time to be in Greece, especially if you watch or take part in the candle-lit Easter processions. Easter is a major holiday for the Greeks so accommodation can be heavily booked.

What to take: Unless you're staying in a good-grade hotel, take a universal plug for the wash-basin. If you like large soft towels in the bathroom, take your own. If you're fastidious you might also want to take an air-freshener for the bathroom.

Pack plenty of insect repellent and your own toiletries and medicines. Take a torch. There's not much street lighting outside the centre of the main towns. You'll be glad of comfortable flat shoes for tramping round historical sites and along dusty uneven beach paths and unmade roads.

Eating out: Most people will have heard that Greek cooking doesn't rate as one of our planet's great cuisines. But lingering for hours under the stars by the edge of the water on a hot evening, with the wine warmer than the salad and the salad warmer than the meat, is truly one of the great holiday experiences.

There's a lot of coast in Greece but not much fish: not to eat in restaurants anyway. Anything other than squid and octopus can be very expensive. If fish is available it will be priced by the kilo and you need to pick out how much you want and check what it will cost before it hits the grill. Otherwise you could be in for an unexpectedly hefty bill.

Menus with English translations are good for a laugh. However many items there are on a menu, only the ones with a price marked will be available. It's quite OK to wander inside and see what's on display or, in more rural places, what's cooking in the pots, before you choose what to eat.

Greek food is served warm, not hot, and your courses are not necessarily served in order.

Greek coffee comes in tiny cups. It's thick and syrupy and the bottom half-inch is coffee grounds. For medium-sweet ask for *metrio*. Leave the cup to stand a minute or so before drinking so that the grounds can settle and don't ever stir it.

'Ordinary' coffee is available just about everywhere there are tourists. Ask for a 'Nes' or an 'American'.

Tipping: Tips aren't demanded. In tavernas you can leave some coins for the waiter in the saucer the bill came on. If there was a junior who was supposed to bring you bread and cutlery leave some coins on the table for him.

Shopping: Most souvenirs have set prices. It is possible to try some friendly haggling for lower prices at souvenir stalls. You'll soon know the sellers who will bargain and those who won't.

There are two postage rates for postcards, for large and small ones. Make it clear which you want when you buy stamps.

'Tourist offices': Many shops selling excursions and tickets, hiring mopeds and changing money call themselves Tourist Offices but they don't belong to the National Tourist Office.

If you see a policeman with a Union Jack stitched to his shoulder, he's a member of the tourist police and can speak English.

• Holland

Holland is an easy place for a holiday. There's no remarkable wild natural scenery or steamy hot beaches but the country is neat and tidy (as long as you overlook the dog problem in Amsterdam) and its tourism set-up is efficient and well run. Most Dutch people speak English and their food and water don't cause horrible stomach problems.

It's not a country that crows loudly about its tourist attractions – which means that the canals and the pretty chiming bells of Amsterdam and Holland's charming 'toy-town' villages and towns come as a lovely surprise to first-time visitors.

Language: The Dutch have long since given up the idea that anyone might learn their language, so they learn other people's. Just about everyone in the cities and towns speaks English, and several other European languages besides. It's polite to ask. 'Do you speak English?' before you start a conversation – even though you know the answer.

Eating and drinking: There are no great bargains but in bars and cafés you won't be shooed away if you want to linger for a long time over your drink.

The ethnic eating experience in Holland is a *rijstafel*, an Indonesian 'rice table'. If you've not tried it, it's quite like Chinese food only spicier and comes with many dishes. The restaurants in Amsterdam are used to tourists and during the holiday periods you need to book. Your hotel will give you suitable numbers and if you telephone, you'll find they will almost certainly speak English.

Tipping: The Dutch attitude to tipping is pretty casual. Taxi meters include a service charge, although tourists often round up the price. Most people leave a tip in restaurants even when a service charge is included. In bars it's the custom to leave a few coins in the saucer that your change comes on. You won't be hounded if you don't.

Bike hire: In Amsterdam the bikes you hire don't have brakes on the handlebars. Instead you have to back-pedal to stop.

Girl talk: Amsterdam's famous red-light district is definitely on the tourist trail, and you needn't feel threatened or at risk if you choose to visit. At night, stick to the well lit streets. They'll be full of other tourists, most of whom have no intention of buying. I've seen plenty of families take children round. 'Mummy, why has that lady not got her dress on? Why is she waving to Daddy?'

Culture on the cheap: If you plan to visit a lot of museums and galleries during your stay, consider buying a museum card. You get them by post from the tourist office in London (Netherlands Service Centre for Tourism, Eggington House, 25–28 Buckingham Gate, London SW1E 6LD) and use them in Holland to visit most museums and galleries for free. In 1989 the card cost £4.50 for under-twenty-sixes and £9.00 for the twenty-six plus. Entry to the major galleries in Amsterdam costs around £2. Cardholders have to pay to see any special temporary exhibitions.

Leisure saver: There is also a leisure card you can buy in Britain (£7.50 in 1989) which gives discounts on some accommodation, some sightseeing excursions, car hire and one day rail-passes, as well as ten per cent off the museum card.

Duty-free? Schiphol Airport – which is midway between Amsterdam and the Hague – has worked hard on its reputation as the airport with the best duty-free buys. Even so, if you plan some serious buying at the airport, check out the best local high-street prices before your holiday.

Independents: If you want to organise a holiday to Holland and not buy a package, the Netherlands Reservations Centre (NRC) organises booking for most sorts of accommodation from youth hostels to luxury hotels, and theatre tickets. They don't charge a service fee. If you telephone Holland on 010 31 70 20 25 00 their high-tech system will recognise that your call is from Britain and you will be answered by someone speaking English.

• India

Who'd have thought even five years ago that we could be jetting off to India for a beach holiday? Yet now you can fly over to Goa to tan on the lovely sandy beaches where a couple of decades ago hippy drop-outs squatted to find peace and love.

Even so, India is mainly a country to visit for sightseeing. Rajasthan is the most popular area for tours and especially good for first-timers, with its stunning palaces and temples to visit, and some high-standard hotels to wallow in.

In India you feel that you are a traveller not a tourist – even when you're shuffling in a queue round famous calendar covers like the Taj Mahal or the palaces of Rajasthan. India, with its riches, its poverty, its crowds and its serenity, gets to you. It's quite normal to come home talking of souls and spirituality. And of diarrhoea.

Doing it by the book: This is a country that loves bureaucracy. It's the great legacy the British gave to India and it was well taught. Just wait till you visit a bank to change some money. Booking into a hotel also involves much form-filling – and on many tours you book into a different hotel every other day. At the end of a trip you will know your passport details off by heart.

Health: Not for nothing do tourists the world over talk of the Delhi belly. Don't drink the water and don't take ice in your drinks or eat locally made ice-cream. Be especially careful about water during the monsoon season when it's at its most contaminated. Be very wary of eating from street stalls, and from buffet tables and restaurants where the food has been on display for some time and the flies are feasting too.

Take a tip from the Indians and, in fierce heat, cool down with warm tea, not ice-cold drinks. Cold drinks supped in the heat cause stomach cramps.

If you suffer from diarrhoea and sickness, be very careful that you don't become dehydrated. Keep drinking a lot of fluid – but not alcohol or tap water. (Study carefully the notes on health on pages 115/123. Most of them apply to India.)

Loss of face: Be wary of stepping out of line and causing offence. I once arrived in Delhi where I was supposed to be met by an official from the tourist office. A bureaucratic cock-up meant that the office wasn't expecting me till the next day. 'No problem,' I said to the man at the tourism desk. 'I'll grab a taxi, go to my hotel and meet up with my host tomorrow.'

This most certainly was not to be. I'd been promised someone would meet me on arrival and therefore I must be met. I was politely and very earnestly asked to wait. So as not to cause offence and 'loss of face' to the official who failed to organise my meeting, I politely and patiently did wait. For an hour and a half. Then the guide arrived, welcomed me and escorted me to my hotel. The journey took ten minutes.

Ask the right questions: The Indians you will meet on your travels will all have the endearing quality of wanting to please you. This should be very good news but it leads to fraught and serious breakdowns in communication. Let's say you ask the question, 'Is the exhibition going to be open tomorrow?' with a look that says you hope it will be. The answer will be: 'Oh, yes, of course.' Saying yes will make you happy, so yes is the answer.

You should have asked the question: 'When will this exhibition be open?' This will no doubt prompt the answer: 'When would you like it to be open?' Stand your ground. Don't give a hint of when you want it to be open or you'll be told that that is when it opens. And when you do finally get an answer to the question, check it with someone else.

Money: You're not allowed to import or export Indian rupees. When you change money make sure you get a currency exchange form, which you will need if you want to change Indian money back into sterling before you leave. The form-filling involved in changing money can take for ever, so at the beginning of the trip you'll save time if you change large-ish amounts.

Dress: Don't show too much flesh – either to the mosquitoes or to the Indians. Men in shorts are usually accepted. Women are expected to dress more modestly.

Tipping: Tipping in India is often not done as a thank-you for a good service rendered but in order to get something done. You don't need to tip taxi-drivers or tip in small restaurants, although these days tourists are expected to. It's wise to tip if you're going to be using a restaurant, or the doorman who gets you a taxi, again. When you return the next day, they won't have forgotten.

Begging: Every traveller has difficulty coming to terms with the poverty you see in India. It's especially harrowing because you step out of your rather luxurious hotel with its buffet groaning with uneaten food and then step over a family of pitiful thin creatures living in the road and surviving on heaven knows what food.

If, as no doubt you'll want to, you give them some money, you'll find yourself surrounded by dozens of others pleading with you for money. There's no feasible way you can give money to every beggar you meet. In India, unlike some other countries, you won't find yourself being cursed and scowled at if you leave them empty-handed. More likely the children will still smile and wave you goodbye.

Life can become easier – and so will your conscience – if instead of handing out coins here and there, you instead send a cheque at the end of your visit to a reputable organisation working in India. When you're there you will find local charities advertised. Or you can wait till you get home and post your cheque to someone like Oxfam, Save the Children or War on Want. Send a note with your money asking that it goes towards a project in India.

You will feel more comfortable walking around the streets if you dress very plainly. Either leave the jewellery and flash watch at home or save them for dinners in the hotel.

Duty-free: Alcohol is expensive in India. You are allowed to bring 0.95 litres of spirits into the country per adult

Tea and coffee: You will be surprised as I was to discover that outside the hotels, and especially in the south, it's hard to get a decent cup of tea! The rural way to serve tea is to boil it up in a pan with milk and sugar. Locally grown coffee, however, is very good.

And finally: The word 'doolally', meaning mentally skewiff, was coined by British soldiers serving in India. If you're on your own for some days in India and you find the country and the customs getting to you, be comforted by knowing that many great writers travelling in India on their own felt by chapter three that they were losing their grasp on reality.

● Ireland

Is the Republic of Ireland abroad or not? It's confusing. Visitors from Britain can have a duty-free allowance yet you don't need a passport. Once, just as I was revving up to drive off the car ferry at Dublin, the English family in the car next to me asked what side of the road they would have to drive on.

Passports: British citizens don't need a passport to travel into the Irish Republic. If you plan to cross the border into the British enclave known as Northern Ireland, it's a good idea to have some identification (passport or driving licence) to show when you meet a spot check at the border.

Duty-free: You are entitled to the EC duty-free allowances. Wines and spirits are expensive in Ireland so it's worth taking in some duty-frees. You do have to pass through customs.

Currency: Irish money is the same as ours, except different. They use pounds and pence, and the coins come in the same denominations and same sizes as ours, except for their 20p piece which is bigger than ours, and they still use a pound note, not a coin. The Irish pound, known as the 'punt', is usually worth slightly less than a pound sterling. Most shops and pubs are prepared to take sterling at face value instead of Irish money. Well, they would, wouldn't they? They make about ten per cent on the deal.

Animals: You can take your family pet to and from Ireland without them needing to stay in quarantine.

Driving: As the English family discovered, you drive on the left as at home. Irish jokers, however, will be the first to tell you that on the country roads you drive in the middle. They're not wrong.

The other Irish motoring quip is that Ireland is the slowest country in Europe – and that's official. There's a maximum speed limit in the Republic of 55 m.p.h. (88 k.p.h.). Distances can be signposted in miles or kilometres. As a rule, unless the sign says kilometres, it's miles.

In some *Gaeltacht* areas – mainly in the west – where the Irish language is still spoken, signposts are in Irish. It's best to know in advance the Irish name for the town or village you're heading for. Mind you, I never worry about getting lost in the Republic. Whoever you meet will try to help you with useful directions – often along the lines of 'Turn left two miles before you get to the church'.

Driving in Ireland is pretty easy but car hire is not cheap, nor is petrol.

● Italy

You won't have the cheapest holiday of your life in Italy. You might come home frazzled by the heat and bleary-eyed from an overdose of art. You might never come to terms with their overpriced, over-regimented beaches and the impromptu chaotic strikes and closures, but the noisy vitality of the Italians, the classical splendour of the countryside and the sights to see make Italy worth visiting again and again and again.

Slow drinks: Don't plan on a quick cup of coffee anywhere near a famous sight. It'll cost you a fortune. Instead, plan your drink for when you fancy a long sit-down. In places like St Mark's Square in Venice or near the Colosseum in Rome, you'll be paying up to £3 for your cuppa but you'll have one of the most famous views in the world to linger over and you won't be hustled to leave your table quickly.

For a quick drink and/or snack, pick a bar without a view and stand at the bar. You pay less than for sitting at a table.

Café tickets: In some self-service snack bars, motorway cafés and bars where you can stand to drink and eat, you first have to pay for what you want, collect a till receipt and then collect your order.

Sunday lunch: The Italians love lunching out on Sundays – the whole family. That means you need to book a table in advance if you want to do the same at a restaurant that's popular with the locals.

Tipping: A service charge of around fifteen per cent is

nearly always added to restaurant bills, but it's customary to leave an extra five to ten per cent for the waiter (it's not done to tip the restaurant owner). You are required by law to obtain an official receipt that shows the sales tax (IVA). In theory the police have the right to stop you as you leave a restaurant and fine you if you haven't got the receipt.

Taxi-drivers, hotel porters, tour guides, waiters and lavatory attendants all expect a tip. So do the staff in the grander hotels – see the general notes on tipping. Drivers and guides reckon on ten to fifteen per cent. Porters expect L1500 a bag; maids L1000 a day (at least) and probably L500 for the person in the loo.

Bills: An all-inclusive price (*tutto compreso*) will include a service charge but not necessarily the sales tax, the IVA. Check this out when you are negotiating the price of a hotel room.

Watch the hidden extras in restaurants. As well as the sales tax, a cover charge (*coperto*) will be added.

Opening hours: You'll soon learn the word *chiuso* – 'closed'. You'll see it on all sorts of museums, galleries, churches and historical sites that you expected to find open. The Italians are prone to close things at the drop of a hat – for restorations, for religious holidays, or for no apparent reason.

Museums and galleries close early – at four o'clock, or three or even two. They're usually closed all day Monday. Churches are often closed to tourists from noon to three or later. Local shops can close for a long lunch.

When there's so much to see and so little time to see it all, as soon as you arrive find out from your hotel, your holiday rep or the tourist office just what is open and when.

Driving: Italian police fine on the spot. They can be hot on speeding, and on drinking and driving. You're not allowed to drive on undipped headlights in towns and cities. In tunnels, however well lit they are, you have to drive on dipped headlights.

You can buy petrol coupons and motorway toll vouchers

before you leave home. (Buy them from the Italian State Office in London or from the AA or RAC.) You are paying the money in advance but you do get a discount and you also become entitled to some free help from the Italian Automobile Club (ACI) if you break down. If you need them you have to phone 116.

Italian two-star petrol 'Normal' is below our equivalent grading so it's better to use only their four-star 'Super'.

Children: Children are seen and heard everywhere in Italy. Never be afraid to take them with you to restaurants – and if yours are blonde you'll be embarrassed at how much cooing and clucking they receive from doting waitresses and waiters.

• New Zealand

New Zealanders are wonderfully hospitable. Perhaps it's because they appreciate the great distances most visitors have to travel for a holiday in New Zealand. From Britain the journey is 14,000 miles yet nowadays nearly half the British who visit the country for a holiday don't have friends or relatives over there. New Zealand offers stunning scenery with just about every form of landscape except true desert. It's pretty quaint too. Gardens are still measured in perches and on Sundays most pubs and shops are closed. However the kilometre has replaced the mile and credit cards are recognised in most places. Just about every small town has a tourist office.

- Unlike Australia, you don't have to apply for a special visa unless you plan to stay longer than six months. A ten-year British passport is enough to get you in.
- You can drive in New Zealand on a British driving licence. And they drive on the left. On the North Island the roads are well maintained and empty. They are not in such good condition on the South Island. The standard of driving in New Zealand is pretty low and there is a high accident rate. Maybe it's because the local drivers aren't used to meeting other cars.
- Don't try to take any food into the country. Leave any picnic leftovers on the plane and ignore your long-lost family's request for a Harrods Christmas cake. New Zealanders are rightly serious about protecting their agriculture from imported disease. Visi-

tors sporting dubious-looking straw hats have been known to have them thoroughly sprayed before they're allowed out of the airport.

- Joy of joys: tipping is virtually unknown in New Zealand.
- Expect prices to be as high as London. New Zealand prices are higher than Australian prices.
- Travel with good medical insurance. British visitors are entitled to some free medical treatment but you pay to see a doctor and for some medicines. Without insurance you would have to cover the cost of any extras incurred flying home.
- Three-quarters of the country's population lives on the North Island. The difference between the North and South Islands is rather like the North and South differences in Italy. The north has the population and the industry. The South is more rural and emptier. New Zealand's South Island is also wetter. Take rain gear.
- On the undeveloped west coast of the South Island insect repellent is a must. The scenery is beautiful but the pesky sand flies live there too and they like nothing better than to feast on tourist flesh.
- The distance between the North and South Islands is similar to the English Channel and the crossing can be as rough.
- Don't underestimate the distance between Australia and New Zealand. New Zealand is 1200 miles south-east of Australia so flying between the two countries takes as long as the flight from London to Athens.

• Portugal

For a country that's just tucked into the edge of the bottom corner of Spain, Portugal is quite un-Spanish. The long strip of coast in the south – the Algarve – is known and visited by millions of Britons who play on the golf courses, wallow in the luxury villas, swim in the breezy Atlantic and pack themselves like the local sardines into the purpose-built holiday apartment blocks.

Language: Portuguese looks a bit like Spanish when it's written down, but sounds nothing like it. Along the Algarve most locals speak some English but, as much of the holiday accommodation is self-catering flats and villas and there are many supermarkets, language is rarely a problem.

Complaints: Every public place, including hotels and restaurants, has to have an official complaints book that is occasionally inspected by the tourist authorities. If you want to make your point about a complaint, demand the *libro de reclamacoes*.

Tipping: Some restaurants include a ten per cent service charge. If they don't, don't withhold a tip just because the service is slow – that's the Portuguese style. They believe that holidaymakers should be relaxed and meals shouldn't be rushed.

Taxi drivers expect a token tip. Most of them won't grumble if it's just a few coins: ten per cent is very generous.

Petrol: There are few petrol stations off the beaten track. If you're driving, keep your tank topped up.

Golf: There's a good selection of golf courses along the Algarve but they are well used and heavily booked.

• Spain

Snobs despise Spain because of all they've read about the busiest resorts. True, if it wasn't for the sun, the licensing hours and the hangovers, there are places in Spain where you hardly feel that you're abroad. However, six miles inland from any part of the coast – including Benidorm, Torremolinos and the island of Majorca – you'll come face to face with a wild and lovely foreign country.

Holidaymakers who have been flying to the Spanish beaches year after year don't need me to tell them what to take, what to do and what to avoid. But if you've never been, or you're thinking of exploring beyond the usual beer'n'chips resorts, here are some things that are useful to know.

Duty-free: Don't buy any duty-free alcohol on the journey from Britain. You'll find everything you could want – and more – for sale in Spain, and at prices less than British duty-free.

I once met some reps in Benidorm who use the local gin to clean their plastic noticeboards. It's cheaper than Flash.

Hotels: If you have a problem with a hotel or restaurant, your best move is to take the matter up with your tour rep (see pages 232/233). However, in Spain all hotels and restaurants must have a supply of official complaint forms and must produce them on demand. They come in triplicate and, if you demand one, you should describe the nature of your complaint (obviously it's best to get it written in Spanish) and send one copy to the Ministry of Tourism, keep one yourself and give one to the people you're complaining against. Just asking a manager for a complaint form can sometimes be enough to get things put right. Ask for a *hoja de reclamaciones*.

Papers: Officially you are supposed to carry your identification papers with you at all times. Not a lot of tourists know that! There is a high theft-rate in Spain and it's foolhardy to carry your passport around with you when it could be locked up in a hotel safe. If you're travelling away from the busy tourist areas, it's better to carry a photocopy of the opening pages of your passport.

Eating out: Restaurants (not cafés that serve meals) are classified by a fork system. Five forks is top of the range and the forks are awarded more for facilities than the standard of food. A five-fork place will offer all the fancy trimmings but not necessarily better food than a much cheaper two-fork restaurant where Spaniards eat.

The Spanish eat later than we do. Lunch needn't start till two o'clock and supper, nine o'clock at the earliest. However, holiday hotels, fast-food places and tourist cafés are tuned to the earlier British times.

In cities Thursday is a big night for dining out. On Fridays the Spanish yuppies head for their weekend apartments. You might need to book a table in advance for Thursday in a restaurant that's popular with the locals.

- In town and city bars your bill is less if you stand at the bar. Eating and drinking at a table costs more.
- Beware the difference between *gazpacho* and *gazpachos*. Without the 's' it's a cold vegetable soup. With the 's' it's a hearty Costa Blanca meat stew.
- Beware the cost of lobster. The price on the menu will be the price per kilo, not per lobster.
- Tipping is by no means obligatory. Restaurant bills include taxes and service but it's customary to leave a tip as well: ten per cent is more than enough. In bars and cafés people usually leave some coins.

Wine: Spanish wines are not all cheap gut-rot. Some are very fine indeed, and much cheaper in Spain than you can buy here. Riojas are considered to be the best red wines, with Rioja Alta the best area. The Penedes area is reckoned to produce very good whites. Torres is the leading Spanish brand for both red and white. If you're not up to making decisions on holiday (or you're just watching the pesetas) ask for the house wine, *vino de la casa*.

Be warned that Sangria – a cocktail of red wine, diced fruit and brandy, served by the jugful – comes in different strengths, from a pleasant thirst-quenching punch to lethal knock-out drops. Sangria made with cheap rough brandy packs a punch. If in doubt, dilute your glass with soda water. There's no truth in the rumour that on those mass-market tourist barbecues, Sangria is mixed with nail polish remover. It just tastes like it.

The cheapest Spanish 'champagnes' are sweet. (The first time I went to Spain in the days of pre-EC prices, I was so knocked out by how cheap the bubbly was, I cleaned my teeth with the stuff just for the hell of it.) If you want a drier, and costlier, fizz look for the word *Brut* on the label.

Fiestas: The Spanish love their fiestas – any excuse to dress up and party. Pick up the free brochure called Festivals of Interest to Tourists – *Fiestas de Interes Turistico* – from a tourist office in Spain. It lists the current year's festivals and when you can catch the processions.

Driving in Spain: By law drivers who hold a green UK driving licence are supposed to have an International Driving Permit or an official Spanish translation of their licence stamped by a Spanish Consulate. In practice you don't need this if you hire a car. If you're stopped by police, the Spanish contract of hire is adequate.

The police can – and do – fine on the spot for motoring offences. These include reckless driving, driving too close to the car in front, drinking and driving, speeding and using full – not dipped – headlights in a built-up area.

Outside built-up areas, and on the Madrid ring road, seat-belts are compulsory for the driver and front-seat passenger.

Outside built-up areas, flash your headlights when you overtake. Some Spaniards hoot their horns instead.

Parking – *aparcamiento* – is pretty haphazard but you are not supposed to park facing oncoming traffic, near junctions or bus-stops, or on main roads. In cities with a blue zone system – *zona azul* – you are limited to stays of 1½ hours and you have to get a disc from the tourist office or the town hall.

In your own car: If you are taking your own car to Spain, it's not compulsory but it is wise to take a Green Card to top up your own insurance policy. (See the chapter on paperwork for drivers.) You should also buy a Bail Bond. Again, it's not compulsory but, after an accident, it will prevent your car being impounded and you being jailed until liability and guilt is sorted out. The AA warn that a Bail Bond might not be recognised by the authorities unless you also have a Green Card.

- You must carry a set of replacement bulbs in the car.
- It is forbidden to carry petrol in a can in a car.

Shopping

- Most shops close for the siesta from 2.00 or 2.30 p.m. to 4.30 or 5.00 p.m.
- Sale signs, *Rebajas*, are seldom genuine – or rather, they stay up all year.
- Banks usually open from 9.00 to 2.00 p.m. Mondays to Fridays and 9.00 to 1.00 p.m. Saturdays.
- Gypsies expect you to bargain with them over prices. Market stallholders and shopkeepers don't.
- Check souvenir toys you are buying for young children and babies. They don't always conform to British safety standards. Check that there are no sharp edges and that soft toys don't have eyes fixed in with dangerous sharp pins.
- If you buy the postcards with embroidered pictures or real lace glued on, you must post them in an envelope. If you don't you'll be exceptionally lucky if they ever arrive.

Self-catering: You can buy most of what you need in the popular resorts, but there are some family favourites that the Spanish just don't seem to do right. At Gatwick, I once asked families checking in for a Spanish charter flight what they had in their hand luggage. Every family that was going on a self-catering trip, and who had been to Spain before, carried a cool-bag with packets of bacon and jars of salad cream.

Cover up: Even in the most touristy resorts, women visiting a church should cover up their shoulders.

Weather-wise: Don't let the pictures in the brochures lull you into thinking it is always hot everywhere in Spain. You'll need a cover-up for evenings except in high summer. The lusher the countryside, the more it rains.

Salty water: When it gets very hot along the Costa Blanca, the water table drops and tap water can get salty. Salty water doesn't lather up. In a drought, if you want serious bubbles you'll need special salt-water soap.

Closing day: Most monuments, museums and serious restaurants are closed on Monday.

● Turkey

If you truly mean it when you say you want a beach holiday 'somewhere different', head for Turkey. If, however, you like your locations to come with five-star mod cons, then don't.

Turkey offers a beautiful coastline, cheap and interesting eating and shopping, and astonishing historical sights. Plumbing and organised entertainment, however, are in their infancy. The busier resorts are well on their way to becoming internationalised but the bar-owner's cousins are still spinning yarn under the olive trees and I haven't yet met a Turk who's interested in bingo. For a whiff of the Orient and a relaxed beach-life, catch Turkey before we sun-seeking Europeans change it too much.

What to take with you

- All the toiletries, medicines, film and tanning creams you might need. You may see film for sale in the resorts but it can often be old. There's often not much choice of suntan creams.
- An effective insect repellent, reliable medicines for stomach upsets and diarrhoea, and tissues.
- A universal plug for the sink. Take towels too. In all but the best hotels, the towels are the size of face-flannels.
- If you intend touring around, buy your map in Britain.

What to wear: Don't take smart expensive clothes unless

you're staying in a very swish hotel. All the resort cafés and restaurants are casual and everywhere gets very dusty.

Take comfortable flat walking-shoes for scrambling round the historical sights. The streets can be obstacle courses too, and as for the pavements – what pavements? Take plastic shoes for swimming off the rocks and off some of the beaches. Stepping on a sea urchin is very painful.

In Istanbul and other large cities, especially in the mosques, women should cover their shoulders and their legs down to the knees. Carry a large lightweight scarf as a cover-up. Men shouldn't attempt to visit a mosque topless or in skimpy shorts.

Health: There are no compulsory inoculations required for entering Turkey but the Department of Health recommends typhoid and cholera jabs.

Don't drink the local water. Bottled water is cheap but always check that the seal hasn't been tampered with.

Money: You get a better exchange rate in Turkey than in Britain. There are banks at the airports for changing sterling and traveller's cheques. Keep the bank receipts. You need them for changing money back before you fly home. Street hawkers offer illegal black-market rates and, obviously, you've no comeback if you get ripped off.

Some of the shops which sell carpets or leather coats accept credit cards, but you'll always get a better price if you offer cash.

Shopping: Tour reps are usually on a commission deal from the carpet and leather shops they recommend. But that doesn't mean that these shops are no good. If you plan to buy an expensive rug, then read up on the different styles and the differences between hand-made and factory-made ones. (The rule for hand-made carpets is: the more knots per square inch, the better the carpet and the more expensive.)

Buying more than a tiny £10 rug is a serious business and involves much straight-faced haggling and tea-sipping.

(Just because you've accepted the shopkeeper's offer of tea, there's no obligation to buy anything.)

Good-value buys include pots of local honey (take it home well wrapped in plastic bags – even the tins leak), sponges, decorated plates, and pistachio nuts; and, of course, wonderful Turkish Delight. The Turkish say, 'Eat sweet, speak sweet'. The local advice is to go for the plain pink and green varieties. The nutty ones, they tell me, may also contain the odd crunchy insect.

The fake 'Lacoste' and other designer sports-shirts from around £3 each are fun to buy. Wash them very carefully. Hot washing can make the crocodile's colour run and a spin in the tumble dryer converts the tops into doll's clothes.

Another Turkish delight: A Turkish massage sounds a treat. But before you visit one, find out from other visitors what really goes on. Most are segregated but the one in Fethiye, for example, bundles foreign men and women together with the massage being performed in the middle of the communal room. Every nook and cranny of your naked body is brusquely cleaned and pummelled. Not for the modest or the tender. Instead, look for a barber who offers a head, neck and arms massage with every shampoo. The one I found managed a neat hair trim too – all for £1.

Shower early: Most accommodation has a solar-heated water system. You need to be back early from the beach, certainly before sunset, to be sure of a warm wash.

Taste tip: If you're planning to go off the beaten holiday track and you don't like thick syrupy Turkish coffee, take your own jar of instant.

And finally: Keep your insect repellent with you for the journey home. The biting armies have fun feasting on the flesh waiting at the airport for the late-night charter flights.

Don't plan to go to work the morning you get home. Those night flights are tedious and exhausting.

The carpet-sellers are quick to offer you a receipt for customs showing a lower price than the one you paid. However, when I took a rug and its receipt through the

Red channel, the first question I was asked was: 'Yes, but what was the real price?'

Turkey is not in the EC, so you can only bring home £32-worth of goods duty-free (other than scents, tobaccos and alcohol).

● Yugoslavia

Yugoslavia has been a quietly popular holiday destination for us British for some time, even though it's not always the first country that springs to mind when you think of foreign holidays. The purpose-built holiday hotels on the coast rarely win points for imaginative or charming design, but most first-time visitors are impressed by the traditional old towns and the coastal scenery. The Yugoslavs like to tell you how they have seven frontiers, six republics, five nations, four main religions, three languages and two alphabets.

Passport: Although it's a Communist country, and not a member of the European Community, it's possible to enter Yugoslavia for a holiday with just a British Visitor's passport. You're issued with a Tourist Pass at the border, which is valid for a month and can't be renewed. Check with your holiday company or travel agent before you leave.

Money: There's a standard rate of exchange everywhere – banks, hotels, post offices and tourist offices, so you're spared the tedious chore of shopping around for the best buys. You rarely have to pay a commission.

If you happen to be coming from Greece, you'll find that you can't change Greek 1000–drachma notes for Yugoslavian dinars.

Petrol: In Yugoslavia you can buy dinar tourist cheques at the border or at banks and tourist offices in the country. They offer a discount on the price of petrol and you use them like cash. They are not refundable if you lose them.

Beaches: Many Yugoslav beaches are rocky or pebbly, with not much sand. Even when they are sandy (these are the ones that get crowded in the summer) there's a noticeable shortage of sunbeds. If you intend to laze on beaches, take a li-lo or at least a mat.

Swimming: In indoor swimming pools, bathing hats – for men as well as women – are often compulsory.

In high season (July and August) most hotels close their indoor pools.

Tipping: Tipping is not obligatory but in restaurants diners often leave an extra ten per cent.

Drinks: Local wines and spirits are much cheaper than imported ones. A bottle of wine bought with a meal in a hotel costs a lot more than a bottle from a supermarket because of the hefty tax the hoteliers have to pay.

There is plenty of tea and coffee in Yugoslavia but it is costly to buy. Packets brought from home make good gifts and thank-you presents.

Illness: British visitors can get free medical help as long as you show your passport. There's a small charge made for any drugs or medicines you are prescribed. But don't forget that without medical insurance you would have to pay dearly if – heaven forbid – you need to come home early or come home on a stretcher. See page 62 and the insurance travel tips.

Souvenirs: In souvenir shops that don't show any prices, you can often bargain over the price you pay.

• When Things Go Wrong

'I Wouldn't Care But Even the Cockroaches Were Rude'

We all deserve holidays that are 110 per cent successful. Many of them are. And when things aren't completely perfect it isn't always because you've been short-changed by the holiday company. A trip can be spoilt by bad weather, impromptu strikes or spending long days and nights with someone you discover you don't much like after all. In cases like this, you can hardly scream for compensation from the tour operator. However, there are other things that can spoil a holiday when they shouldn't.

The times they are a-changing . . . What can you do if your holiday company changes the particulars of your holiday at short notice?

You sensibly booked your holiday, months in advance, because you want to fly out on a Saturday from your local airport. Then, lo and behold, two weeks before the off, you get a letter telling you that you're now flying from a different airport and on Friday not Saturday. Is there anything you can do about it?

The Association of British Travel Agents (ABTA) has a Code of Conduct which covers tour operators who are members. It says that any company that changes your holiday in a significant way must tell you without delay, and they must give you the choice of accepting the change or having your money refunded in full. What often happens in practice, of course, is that you have no choice but to accept because there's not enough time to find another holiday you want.

If this happens to you, accept the change in writing but

say that you are only accepting *under protest*. If you think they made a major change – different hotel, different departure days, different airport – you can try to claim for compensation once you get back home. (See later in this chapter for how to go about it.)

There are still plenty of unpleasant things that might happen which you can't claim compensation for. The small print always explains that the tour company is not liable for changes caused by 'war, riots, civil strife, terrorist activity, industrial disputes, natural disasters, fire, technical problems to transport, closure of airports or ports, changes to airline schedules, cancellation of flights and similar events beyond our control'. Which seems to cover most things. There is talk of all this changing come 1992.

Charge of the heavy brigade: When you first choose your holiday and pay the deposit you might think that you know how much the thing is going to cost. It ain't necessarily so. Buried among the small print on the booking form, you'll probably find that the company reserves the right to increase the price of your holiday before you leave. They can, and they do – often at the last moment, so again you don't have much option but to accept.

The question of surcharges has been hotly debated in the travel business in recent years. It has been claimed that some companies slap them on willy-nilly, as a way of making extra profits. The companies retort that if their costs go up suddenly, they shouldn't have to bear the brunt and make a loss on your holiday. Some tour operators had a spell of claiming 'Definitely no surcharges' . . . then quietly dropped the idea.

The ABTA Code of Conduct says that a member company can only add a surcharge for reasons that occur 'beyond their control'. By this they usually mean a big change in the value of the pound or the cost of air fuel. The Code also says that the company must give you, the customer, a 'reasonable written explanation'. If your company asks for extra money after you've booked, you have every right to ask them to explain, in writing, just what it's for. If you're not satisfied and you think they're just using the term 'holiday surcharge' to get some extra cash from you, take up the matter with ABTA, or with your local Trading Standards Officer (at the Town Hall). Otherwise ask for advice at your local Legal Centre or Citizen's Advice Bureau (their numbers are in the phonebook).

When your holiday never happens: 'What did you say was the name of that company we booked with? There's a story here in the paper . . .' What happens if you've paid for your holiday, or paid the deposit for it, and the company stops trading?

If the holiday company is a member of ABTA you will be offered some sort of alternative holiday or, if you prefer, you can have your money refunded. If the company is not a member of ABTA – and some quite reputable companies do not belong, for valid reasons – but it has an Air Tours Organiser's Licence (ATOL) issued by the Civil Aviation Authority (CAA), you will still get your money back.

Even without this cover, you're not completely sunk. It may be that the company had some sort of bonding scheme covering passengers if it should go under. Alternatively, you may have bought a travel insurance policy which covers you against the bankruptcy of your holiday company and will refund your money (see chapter on insurance).

Finally, if you've paid £100 or more for the holiday with a credit card, and you paid it direct to the tour company – not a travel agent – then technically your buying contract is between you and the credit card company. They are obliged to refund your money.

If the company folds when you're away: 'We thought something was up when we saw the rep in tears . . .' The most horrifiying prospect of all is to be away on holiday when you learn that the company that took you there has gone bust. It must be said that this happens very rarely, and in any case, it's not the end of the world – or even necessarily the end of your holiday.

If the company was a member of ABTA or had an ATOL number, your holiday shouldn't be too disrupted when the holiday company folds. This is because ABTA or the CAA will use money deposited with them by members and licence-holders to see that you get home and, whenever possible, that you stay abroad for as long as you booked for.

If your company wasn't covered in this way – basically you're on your own. Again, your insurance policy may cover you, but you won't be able to get a penny out of them until later. Meanwhile, it's up to you to sort things out and get home as best you can. This is when most people rush to the British Embassy or Consulate. But the consular service is at pains to point out that they're not in business to bail out bankrupt holiday companies.

What the Consul can do, if you're genuinely broke, is contact your relatives or friends and ask them to help with money or tickets; advise you on how to transfer funds; in an emergency, cash you a cheque for £50 if you have a bank card; and as a very last resort, make you a repayable loan. But *don't* storm into the Consulate waving your British Passport and expect a free fly-you-home service.

When you are on holiday: 'I wouldn't care but even the cockroaches were rude . . .' As a nation, we win medals for suffering in silence. If your holiday turns out not to be the one you were promised, don't just sit there grumbling: you should take action on the spot.

For starters, it helps if you've brought with you your holiday brochure and any letter you were sent, or a copy of the booking form that mentions any special promises. They help you put your case. You should also take with you the phone number of the tour company's head office, in case an angry call is necessary.

But first start with the people on the spot. Begin by complaining politely and with a smile. Be calm but firm. Report your complaint at once to your holiday rep and, if it concerns the hotel, to the hotel manager.

If you've been given the wrong sort of room – perhaps one without a bath and at the back of the hotel, when you ordered (and have proof you ordered) a room with a bath and sea view – see the hotel manager straight away and before you unpack. Even if the hotel is fully booked for the week but newcomers are still checking in, there'll be time to divert you to the one you ordered.

If nothing happens and you are stuck with your problem, make clear, detailed and dated notes of every meeting you have with managers and reps. You can also ask other holidaymakers to sign a statement you've made about what's happening – or isn't. Add their full names and addresses.

Take photographs if they will help your case. They provide evidence that your 'sea view' was the kitchen dustbins and the carpark, or that the 'peaceful relaxing gardens' were planted with concrete-mixers and jack-hammers.

Keep receipts if you have to spend money you hadn't banked on spending. For example, if you can't get the free windsurfing lessons you were promised at your hotel, and you have to travel to another beach and buy them, ask both the sailboard instructor and the taxi driver for some sort of receipt.

Be realistic. A £99 holiday in Spain is never going to offer deluxe accommodation in an exclusive tropical resort and you shouldn't expect it to. After all, it costs nearly that much for two British Rail breakfasts and a standard return ticket from London to Blackpool.

Complaining after the holiday: If nothing happens to put right a reasonable complaint, as soon as you get home go promptly to your travel agent. Show them your tan and tell them your horror story. Some agents will take up your case with the tour operator.

Write on: If the travel agent is unhelpful, or if you booked direct, you should write a clear, short letter to the tour operator. The address is in the brochure. Telephone the company to find out the name of the managing director. It can help to address the letter directly to the MD.

In the letter include your travel dates and where you stayed and, if you have it, your booking reference number. Outline your complaint, what you did about it on holiday and what action you want the company to take. If possible have the letter typed. Date it and keep a copy. Send it with *copies* of letters, photos and statements that back up your complaint. Keep a copy of every letter you send.

Don't cloud the issue with unnecessary whinging about unconnected issues, like the rain or the noisy foreigners in the next bedroom. If you want compensation you should say how much in the letter and add the words 'without prejudice' so that you're not committed to that sum.

You must now be prepared to dig in for a long fight. Some companies don't even have the good manners to reply to letters of complaint. Others send a standard letter of regret. Many seem to believe that if they make no effort, complainers will just melt away. Sadly, prompt and generous replies are as common as tropical heatwaves in Britain. Occasionally a company might offer a small sum or a discount off another holiday in return for you dropping the matter. It's up to you to decide if their offer is sufficient compensation for what you suffered.

Carrying on claiming: If you're not happy with any reply you get and the company is a member of ABTA, you can ask ABTA to act as a go-between for you, using their free conciliation scheme. This sometimes spurs the company into taking your claim seriously, and sometimes it doesn't. Either way, in my experience ABTA is a slow-moving beast that needs a lot of kicking.

If nothing satisfactory comes of conciliation, ABTA also organises an arbitration scheme. An independent arbitrator makes a judgement on your case and you are obliged to settle for what the arbitrator says. The drawbacks here – apart from the time it takes – are that all your evidence has to be presented in writing, which is a chore, and the holiday company has to agree to go to arbitration in the first place. Both you and the company pay a fee (from £23) for this scheme, which is usually returnable to the 'winner'.

Other routes: If the holiday company doesn't belong to ABTA (or won't take part in the ABTA arbitration scheme or if you prefer to keep ABTA out of all this), you can try for legal compensation through the small claims procedure in the County courts in England and Wales. You don't need a solicitor. In fact they're discouraged and if you win you're not allowed to claim their fee. For free legal advice and help with pursuing a complaint, try your nearest Citizens' Advice Bureau or Law Centre. Their numbers are in the phone book.

If you think that the company described the holiday innaccurately in their brochure or in a letter to you, report their empty promises to the Trading Standards Officer in the area where the company's head office is situated (you can get the number of the Town Hall from Directory Enquiries). The Trading Standards Office can take out a criminal prosecution against the company and you could be awarded damages.

As a last resort, if you paid for the holiday with a credit card (as long as it was more than £100 and you paid the company direct, not a travel agent), in theory you can approach the credit card company for compensation. I personally have not heard of any holiday complaints being satisfactorily solved this way – but if all else has failed, it might be worth a try.

Don't try it on: It's simply not worth cooking up a phony complaint, or exaggerating a minor niggle, in the hope of getting some cash. Greedy holidaymakers who try it on only queer the pitch for genuine complainers. Contrary to what you may have heard in the pub, the holiday companies aren't in the business of handing out sacks of money to professional complainers to keep them quiet. Sadly, many of them also try hard not to be in the business of handing out money to holidaymakers with genuine complaints either.

Trudy Culross

IT GETS BETTER AFTER CAIRO

Bold, defiant and thirty-three, twelve progressively painful years of marriage behind her, Trudy Culross had mixed feelings about travelling round the world.

Her decision to go it alone was not an auspicious one. It was met, in fact, by a bruising kickoff that came out of the cloudless blue at Cordoba, followed by a narrow escape from a murderous psychopath in Rome.

But things really did get better after Cairo, though not without incident. A camel ride in Egypt led to a midnight flight from the Bedouin who thought his eyes were on his second wife. And a great many further adventures lay ahead. Learning to treat Nubian lepers with the same respect as Indian maharajahs, she also came to respect the one person she had so long forgotten – herself.

With disarming honesty and humour, Trudy tells of those she met and loved and left behind. Her story is a journey of self-discovery, and each experience a point on the map of her transformation.

'A terrific read – honest, funny and moving.'   *Daily Mail*

'An extraordinary book by an extraordinary woman . . . more enthralling than any adventure novel.'   *Company*

'The ultimate escapist dream, except that every word is true.'
                                                            Today

'Sad, funny and brutally honest . . . I couldn't put it down.'
                                                      Cosmopolitan

Roger Cook and Tim Tate

WHAT'S WRONG WITH YOUR RIGHTS?

Did you know that:
- an Englishman's home is *not* his castle – dozens of people have the right to enter your home without permission?

- by the end of the century a policeman on the beat will have instant access to all your medical, social services, criminal and financial records at the touch of a computer button?

- an unmarried father has no legal rights to his child?

- we have no statutory right to freedom of speech?

This book reveals the *real* situation regarding your rights. Roger Cook and Tim Tate, from Central Television's investigative series *The Cook Report*, dissect our legal system to show how our traditional 'rights' – if they ever existed – are constantly being eroded or threatened.

Drawing on a wealth of case histories and personal tragedies, *What's Wrong With Your Rights?* is a searing indictment of the way government, local councils, the law and big business can legally ride roughshod over the ordinary citizen who pays for their very existence. It is a compelling warning of the dangers of complacency as we go about our daily lives.

'An excellent compendium of oppression'   *Literary Review*

'A grim case-study of how fragile our rights are' *Sunday Express*

Simon Frith

FACING THE MUSIC

What frustrates the rock fans and critics of today is the tenet held by so many of their contemporaries that current music should be measured in terms of what it meant twenty years ago. Now that the 45 r.p.m. record – the symbol of that notion – looks set to go the same way as the 78, the music which so persistently seeks novelty, sensation and change deserves some critical redefinition.

Simon Frith's invigorating anthology fills the void.

Jon Savage suggests that youth, the core market of rock, has won the battle to define its counterculture whilst assimilating itself just as surely into shopcounter commercialism. . .

Mary Harron expounds the idea of pop as a commodity, that hype is not simply the peripheral patter to good music but the crucial vernacular that identifies it. . .

Simon Frith himself assesses the implications of technological and cross-media developments without succumbing to the simplistic lament for lost innocence and authenticity. . .

Further contributions include support for the black cross-over into white sound, and a history and rationale of rock's fundamental institution – the radio. Original and thought-provoking, these essays challenge the accepted constructs of rock ideology.

'Required reading for every music fan who complains that the universe of rock & roll has been reduced to one never-ending jeans commercial.'
                                                                    Metroland

Jane R. Hirschmann
Carol H. Munter

OVERCOMING OVEREATING

Lose weight naturally. Enjoy the food you most desire. Forget
your preoccupation with eating and weight. Discover the
freedom of no restraints. Give up dieting forever.

Overcoming Overeating makes this all possible, for the authors
have returned eating to its natural place in life, so that food
becomes something to be enjoyed rather than feared.

Concentrating on the normal physiological hunger that we all
experience Jane R. Hirschmann and Carol H. Munter help you
to break out of the lonely cycle of diet, binge, recrimination and
self-loathing. Both practical and reassuring, they offer radical,
realistic guidance on how to conquer an obsession and restore
the compulsive eater's self-esteem.

'This is the best book on dealing with compulsive eating that
I've read. The authors themselves are veterans of "mouth
hunger" as opposed to "stomach hunger", and the compassion
and understanding with which they address you, the reader,
magically motivate you to join them in becoming a
noncompulsive eater.' Penelope Russianoff, author, *When Am I
Going To Be Happy?*

Jancis Robinson

THE DEMON DRINK

'Every intelligent drinker owes it to his (and, particularly, her)
liver, and gut, and brain, and children, to find out more about
alcohol and about whether they fall into any of the particularly
high-risk groups, which include such disparate categories as
those with a small frame, an ulcer, high blood pressure, or a job
on a boat.'

Alcohol is our favourite drug. Used properly, it is a pleasure
central to millions of lives. Used unwisely, it can become a
substance more dangerous than most of us realize. As members
of a culture in which alcohol plays such an important part, we
actually know surprisingly little about it.

Hence this book, providing the first genuinely objective and
comprehensive information about exactly how much of a demon
drink really is. Drink can, indeed, be a wonderful thing. The
aim of this book is to celebrate that fact, while placing alcohol
in perspective and, most importantly, encouraging a new respect
for it.

'It's not an anti-alcohol book, more a user's guide to the true
pros and cons of drinking.'   *Daily Mail*

'Jancis Robinson is our cleverest, most thoughtful wine writer.
In *The Demon Drink*, she has anticipated what are certain to
become the most crucial issues for those who really care about
wine . . . It will probably turn out to be one of her most important
books.'   *Observer*

'Beautifully written and awash with sobering facts about alcohol
as part of our lives, the book is nonetheless cheerily encouraging
as to the benefits of modest tippling as well as being
unpatronisingly frank about the all-too-real dangers of overdoing
it.'   *Ideal Home*

David Lewis

HELPING YOUR ANXIOUS CHILD

'Anxiety is a curse which can cast a damaging spell over your child's life. But there is a cure. It is to be found in this book – and in your hands.'

Is anxiety making your child's life a misery – causing problems at school, difficulties in making friends or facing new experiences, even affecting physical health?

Chronic anxiety is a serious problem which may be general, may be a specific anxiety about taking exams or doing sums, or a phobia about anything from trains or spiders to eating in public or going to the toilet. It can, however, be treated successfully, and David Lewis offers practical guidelines to parents of anxious children.

By being 'positive, patient, persistent and prudent', you can transform your child into a happy, confident member of society.

SEX & YOUR HEALTH

Edited by Dr James Bevan

The recent spread of AIDS has brought the relationship between
sex and health to the forefront of public debate. It has also given
rise to a maze of misinformation about sex and sexual problems.

In this book – the first encyclopaedic survey of the subject –
nine experts disentangle the medical facts from the myths and
explain, simply and authoritatively, the physiology and
psychology of sex-related health problems.

* The anatomy and physiology of sex

* Main methods of contraception

* Causes of male and female infertility

* Physical problems that affect sexuality

* Ageing and sexuality

* Sexually transmissible diseases

* The psychology of sex

* Deviation from the sexual norm

* Sexuality in the social context

Hugo Cornwall

DATATHEFT

Datatheft: the undetectable crime that grows wherever new
opportunities exist. The typical computer criminal is not the
genius programmer or hacker, but the middle-ranking,
apparently loyal employee with inside knowledge. Computer
fraud is a problem that goes to the heart of management
responsibility. Read this book – you may never know what
you're missing.

The bestselling author of the controversial *Hacker's Handbook*,
Hugo Cornwall, a computer security consultant, is uniquely
qualified to describe the nature of the crime that has no
discernible parameters. Even in law it is an area of lightest grey.

'Required reading in every computer department in every
company in the country.'
PC Week

A Selected List of Non-Fiction Available from Mandarin

While every effort is made to keep prices low, it is sometimes necessary to increase prices at short notice. Mandarin Paperbacks reserves the right to show new retail prices on covers which may differ from those previously advertised in the text or elsewhere.

The prices shown below were correct at the time of going to press.

☐	7493 0109 0	**The Warrior Queens**	Antonia Fraser	£4.99
☐	7493 0108 2	**Mary Queen of Scots**	Antonia Fraser	£5.99
☐	7493 0010 8	**Cromwell**	Antonia Fraser	£7.50
☐	7493 0106 6	**The Weaker Vessel**	Antonia Fraser	£5.99
☐	7493 0014 0	**The Demon Drink**	Jancis Robinson	£4.99
☐	7493 0016 7	**Vietnam – The 10,000 Day War**	Michael Maclear	£3.99
☐	7493 0061 2	**Voyager**	Yeager/Rutan	£3.99
☐	7493 0113 9	**Peggy Ashcroft**	Michael Billington	£3.99
☐	7493 0177 5	**The Troubles**	Mick O'Connor	£4.99
☐	7493 0004 3	**South Africa**	Graham Leach	£3.99
☐	7493 0254 2	**Families and How to Survive Them**	Creese/Skynner	£5.99
☐	7493 0060 4	**The Fashion Conspiracy**	Nicolas Coleridge	£3.99
☐	7493 0179 1	**The Tao of Pooh**	Benjamin Hoff	£2.99
☐	7493 0000 0	**Moonwalk**	Michael Jackson	£2.99

All these books are available at your bookshop or newsagent, or can be ordered direct from the publisher. Just tick the titles you want and fill in the form below.

Mandarin Paperbacks, Cash Sales Department, PO Box 11, Falmouth, Cornwall TR10 9EN.

Please send cheque or postal order, no currency, for purchase price quoted and allow the following for postage and packing:

UK   80p for the first book, 20p for each additional book ordered to a maximum charge of £2.00.

BFPO   80p for the first book, 20p for each additional book.

Overseas   £1.50 for the first book, £1.00 for the second and 30p for each additional book
including Eire   thereafter.

NAME (Block letters) ....

ADDRESS ....

....

....